STEP-BY-STEP GARDEN GUIDES

Peter McHoy

Pests and Diseases

AURA

Step-by-Step Garden Guides
Pests and Diseases

Peter McHoy

© 1998 Aura Books plc
Produced for Aura Books by
Transedition Limited
Oxford OX4 4DJ, England

This edition published in 2001
by Advanced Marketing,
Bicester, Oxfordshire.

Editing and layout: Asgard
Publishing Services, Leeds

Typesetting: Organ Graphic,
Abingdon

Photographic credits
All photographs by the author.

10 9 8 7 6 5 4 3

Printed in Dubai

ISBN 1 901 683 06 0

Peter McHoy has worked on six gardening magazines, three of them as editor, but now devotes most of his time to writing and photography. He has written more than 40 books, most of them on gardening, and contributes regular gardening features to *Park Homes* and *Practical Householder*. He also runs his own horticultural photographic library and acts as consultant to several publishers.

His interest in gardening goes back to childhood — he can remember the excitement of looking over the hedge and being fascinated by a neighbour's greenhouse full of seedlings in spring. This early enthusiasm sparked a particular interest in seeds, and he became a seed analyst before a change of direction took him into publishing over 30 years ago.

He is equally fascinated by plant pests and diseases, and actually finds it exciting to discover a new one in his garden. On the other hand, he knows only too well the disappointment caused by some of the commoner pests and diseases. Yet he's convinced that, if you put such problems in perspective, they need not spoil the pleasures and joy of gardening.

CONTENTS

Dahlias are vulnerable to pests and diseases, but their magnificent blooms amply repay every effort to protect them from the ravages of blackfly (left inset), earwigs (top inset) and others.

4 Introduction

Striking a balance 4

6 Battle plans

Soft soap or
chemical warfare? 6
Biological warfare 8
Purchasing
predators 11
Know your
predators 12
Sex appeal 16
Traps and pits 17
Putting up barriers 20
Repellents and
scarers 24
Resistant varieties 25

27 Chemical warfare

Insecticides 27
Fungicides 30

32 Strategic planning

Know your enemy 32
No hiding place 34

36 Pests

Identification and
control 36
Roots, bulbs and
tubers 37
Leaf pests 41
Fruit problems 50
Flower problems 53
Stem problems 55

57 Animals and pets

Friend or foe? 57
Dogs and cats 58
Wild mammals 59
Birds 60

64 Diseases

Identification and
prevention 64
Roots, bulbs and
tubers 65
Leaf problems 69
Fruit problems 78
Flower problems 80
Stem problems 81

83 Deficiencies and disorders

Nutritional and
physiological
problems 83
Nutritional
deficiencies 84
Physiological
disorders 86

91 Lawn problems

A healthy lawn 91

95 Index

Striking a balance

There's nothing more exasperating than some garden pest that seems impossible to control. And it can be so frustrating when you put all your efforts into gardening only to be thwarted by a whole series of plant ailments.

If you're familiar with such problems, then this is just the kind of book you need. The aim is to help you not only to control the problems that seem to plague your garden, but also to view them in a more positive light. There's plenty of advice on how to keep your plants healthy, and with luck you'll soon find that pest and disease control can be a challenge that actually adds interest to your gardening.

We hope you find this a positive and constructive book, despite the negative nature of its subject. There's more to coping with plant problems than simple diagnosis and prescription: there are philosophical considerations, judgements to make, and a balance to be struck between benefits and penalties. Pest and disease control can even become one of those stimulating challenges that becomes enjoyable once you've mastered the basic principles.

Chrysanthemums — now more correctly referred to as dendranthemums — are prone to a number of pests such as leaf miners and earwigs. But if you're ready and prepared for them, and act promptly at the first sign of attack, these beautiful flowers can be grown to perfection without even a blemish.

Some gardeners may possess such natural curiosity that they actually *welcome* a new pest or disease in the garden — something new to identify and perhaps photograph. But when their favourite plants come under attack, even the most devoted nature watchers rapidly turn their thoughts to methods of control. It's all a matter of perspective.

Taking a relaxed view

If you worry about every leaf spot that appears, or every insect you can't identify, then gardening will cease to be a pleasure. Try to be relaxed about those problems that don't really matter.

If your forget-me-nots or pansies succumb to mildew shortly before the end of the season, it's not worth spraying them as the plants will soon be pulled up anyway. Just burn them rather than composting them or leaving them lying around, as this will reduce the number of spores that can infect plants next season.

If you notice a little cuckoo-spit on a shrub, then either kill the insects or ignore them if the numbers are low; many of them will probably be picked off by predators anyway.

Not everything that looks serious is anything to worry about. The conspicuous galls caused by lime nail gall mite (see page 44) may look serious, but the tree is unlikely to come to any harm.

A build-up of aphids, on the other hand, requires prompt attention. Not only will they multiply very fast and affect the plant's health and growth, they may also carry virus diseases.

Solomon's seal slugworms (sawfly larvae) will completely strip a plant in a day or two. The plant will live to grow another year, but so will the overwintering population of slugworms unless you kill them while you can still see them on the plant.

Observation and prompt action when it *is* needed will mean you have few persistent problems.

The big debate

Pest and disease control is a subject of controversy and sometimes heated argument. Some consider 'natural' forms of pest control the only acceptable option; others feel reassured by the spray gun or puffer pack, and are unwilling to risk damaging their crops by using methods they consider less certain.

For those who place themselves firmly on one side or the other of this debate, it's important for me to lay my own cards on the table. Personally, I believe in an integrated pest management system, whereby chemicals are only used when other options fail. However, I must confess that when a favourite plant is about to be overwhelmed, I find myself compelled to reach for the pesticide bottle.

The purpose of this book is to offer helpful suggestions whatever your personal beliefs on the subject, and where relevant I have suggested both chemical and more 'natural' methods of control. The question you must resolve in your own mind is whether you use chemicals as the first or last resort.

Soft soap or chemical warfare?

Garden chemicals in perspective

It's important to put garden chemicals in perspective. Modern garden chemicals are far safer than many of those our grandparents used, such as arsenic, mercury, cyanide and nicotine. There were no stringent safety regulations like the ones we have today. Modern garden chemicals should *always* be treated with respect, but we are probably at less risk today than earlier generations of gardeners.

Most of us have potentially dangerous products around the home, including bleach and caustic soda, but many of us are prepared to use them with adequate precautions. Garden chemicals are no different: they have been shown to be safe to use **provided you follow the instructions**.

We should not ignore potential hazards. The fact that many garden chemicals once considered safe are now banned is a salutary reminder that our understanding of them may not always be as complete as we tend to assume. However, scientists nowadays are more aware of such hazards, and testing and safety clearances are rigorous.

Not everything that comes out of a pesticide bottle is blacklisted by those gardeners who regard chemicals with a healthy suspicion. Some chemicals are based on naturally occurring products — pyrethrum and derris, for example, both of which are derived from plant products.

You may also feel more comfortable using 'gentle' chemicals such as those based on soaps — described on the label as fatty acids — rather than the more potent pesticides. These are decisions only you can make.

When it comes to controlling fungal diseases, the options for natural alternatives are more limited, though sulphur and copper products are regarded more favourably by some as they are naturally occurring elements. This doesn't necessarily make them safer or more effective, however.

One of the major problems with insecticides is that they are indiscriminate, killing off the beneficial insects along with the pests. This means that natural pest control becomes ineffective, while vital pollinating insects such as bees may be killed. Pirimicarb is selective in that it kills aphids but not beneficial insects. On the other hand it is dangerous to fish and other aquatic life.

Ladybirds are natural garden predators that feed voraciously on aphids. Visible just above the ladybird are the 'mummified' remains of aphids that have been parasitised by a tiny wasp. The holes in the 'mummies' are where the wasps emerged.

Above
Striking at the first sign of trouble can save a lot of problems in the long term. Small hand sprayers containing ready-mixed insecticides are therefore useful for quick and immediate action. Greenfly have just appeared on this petunia, and need to be dealt with before the population becomes larger and more difficult to control. Such prompt action may mean that fewer chemicals are required in the end.

Left
Here is an example of pest control by purely biological means. A suspension of the bacterium Bacillus thuringiensis *is being prepared to control certain caterpillars (see page 13). The dropper on the left contains washing-up liquid, which will simply be added as a spreader.*

Biological warfare

Biological controls are a fast-expanding method of pest control and the subject of much current research. They will almost certainly become an increasingly important part of the gardener's armoury.

There's nothing new about biological control — the well-known ladybird and its larvae have been chomping their way through aphids for as long as there have been ladybirds — but the importation of predators and parasites from different parts of the world has made it possible to control a wider range of pests, especially under glass. Biological pest control is now widely practised by commercial growers, which is a sure indication of its effectiveness.

Now, thanks to the availability of biological controls in small gardeners' packs, the technique has become a practical possibility for most domestic gardeners. Because, however, they are living creatures, the actual insects are not usually sold directly by garden centres, and are normally sent by post. Also, with the one exception of the bacterium used to control caterpillars (see page 13), they normally have to be released shortly after arrival, so the suppliers usually allow you to state a preferred delivery date.

Biological controls are not a cheap option, and you must be prepared to accept a small population of the pest they prey on. Otherwise they will be deprived of their means of support and will probably die out. Also, some controls are only suitable for the greenhouse or conservatory, or for houseplants in the home. Many of them originate from warm climates, and will die out during the winter months outdoors — a useful reassurance if you are concerned about the uncontrolled spread of introduced species.

Timing is also important if biological controls are to work efficiently. It's no use, for example, introducing them before the pest appears. On the other hand, waiting until the population is very high may mean control is less effective.

A tiny parasitic wasp called Aphidius matricariae *is here being released to control aphids.*

What modern pest control can look like — a kit containing microscopic nematodes that help to control vine weevils.

Commitment

Biological control requires a lot of commitment. If you're impatient and start using chemical sprays before the biological control has had a chance to become effective, then you'll probably wipe out the 'goodies' along with the 'baddies'.

Surveys have also shown that biological control tends to be less successful if you've used insecticides during the preceding months, even if you stop as soon as you introduce the beneficial insects. Some insecticides can be very persistent, so don't judge biological

It's advisable to cover newly intro-duced predators with horticultural fleece or a bug net for a week or two — especially with predators that may fly off — so as to help establish the colony.

control a failure until it's had time to prove itself.

It may also be necessary to restrict the introduced preda-tors to the affected area, perhaps with a special insect-proof net. Some of them will readily take to the wing, and fly off long before you can reap the benefit.

Biological controls are best used as part of an integrated

pest control policy — using resistant plant varieties where appropriate, and applying barrier methods (see page 20), traps and good garden hygiene. If you grow vege-tables, crop rotation helps to prevent a build-up of soil-borne pests and diseases.

It's also worth bearing in mind that strong, healthy plants are less likely to suc-cumb to diseases than weak ones struggling to survive.

Native predators

The food chain is a long and complex one, and biological pest control extends far

9

beyond parasites and predators bought specifically for the purpose. Native wildlife can also help to control pests in your garden, though they may require encouragement in the form of plants that attract them. Yellow flowers, for example, tend to attract hoverflies, the larvae of which devour aphids.

Ladybirds and their larvae are voracious eaters of aphids, and are found in almost every garden (the seven-spot is the best-known, but there are many kinds). Hoverfly larvae are equally effective at keeping down the aphid population, and are equally common.

Neither of these insects will control a heavy infestation that is already established, but they may restrict the population if they are present at the right time. Unfortunately, the pests often start to breed and multiply before the predators are fully active, so chemical control may be more relevant early in the season.

Spraying the aphids is likely to kill the predators too, unless you use one that is reasonably selective, such as pirimicarb. This controls aphids but has little effect against other pests or most beneficial insects, so is the preferred choice if you plan to depend heavily on natural predators.

Many common birds are efficient predators. Blue tits enjoy aphids, while blackbirds and thrushes will help to control slugs and snails. They

have to break open the snail shells, so it may be helpful to provide a few stone 'anvils' for the birds to knock them against. Feeding the birds may also encourage them into your garden. Bear in mind that some species can become pests in their own right: blackbirds, for example, will quickly devour your strawberry or redcurrant crop.

A garden pond will encourage birds and many other kinds of wildlife, including frogs and toads, and these too will help to keep down the slug population.

Such natural predators are unlikely to be present in sufficient numbers to control pests likes slugs and snails completely — even a pondside bed of hostas can have shredded foliage despite the presence of hundreds of frogs! These natural controls should be seen as aids rather than complete solutions.

Hoverflies may look a little like wasps, but they are harmless to humans, and their larvae eat aphids voraciously. If you want to encourage these insects, bear in mind that they are attracted to yellow flowers.

Almost any pond will attract frogs in early spring, and the resulting spawn will ensure a healthy population to control pests such as slugs. But don't expect them to provide a complete solution.

Purchasing predators

Biological controls are only suitable for certain pests, and most of them are very specific in the ones they control. Whereas a broad-spectrum insecticide will control a wide range of pests, if you take the biological route you may have to buy a range of different predators.

Some predators are unsuitable for outdoor use in our climate, but will control some of the most troublesome greenhouse pests, such as whitefly and red spider mite. They are especially useful if you are growing edible crops such as tomatoes, cucumbers and aubergines in the same greenhouse, as there are no pesticide residues to worry about and the crops can be harvested at any time.

Timing is of the essence

It's a waste of money applying a biological control when the pest hasn't appeared yet. The best time for application is when the noxious beasts are present but still vulnerable, either at a particular point in their life cycle or when their numbers are low.

Predatory mites called Phytoseiulus persimilis *have arrived packed in vermiculite and are being released to control red spider mites.*

Buying and applying

Although there are variations according to the type of predator being used, most of them arrive in small non-airtight tubes or sachets. Some will simply be loose in the container, while others may be on a piece of special paper in the tube, and a few may be mixed in with fine vermiculite.

Applying the insect predators is easy. Just open the container and allow them to crawl out over the plants. If there's paper in the tube, pull this out and leave it on the plant, but leave the tube resting on the plant until all the insects are out. Occasionally some of them will 'play dead', but they will move if you leave them for a while.

If they are packed with vermiculite, tip them out onto the surface of the compost and distribute them around a number of plants.

Some predators are large enough to see easily with the naked eye, while others are unlikely to be visible without a hand lens. They will all distribute themselves among the affected plants, though some may be *too* mobile and fly off if not restricted in some way.

In a greenhouse, cover the door and ventilators with an insect-proof mesh, at least for a few days. Alternatively, drape some fleece or a barrier mesh over treated plants. Once the colony has become established, such precautions should be unnecessary, and outdoors they are not practicable anyway.

Eelworms and bacteria

Tiny microscopic nematodes (eelworms) are used to control vine weevils, and a bacterium

Know your predators

These wasps don't sting!

Some of the biological controls discussed in this section are technically wasps, but they don't sting and are harmless to humans! Their effectiveness in controlling pests lies in the fact that they parasitise their victims.

is used against caterpillars. However, both of these creatures are so tiny that they have to be mixed with water and then watered or sprayed on. Always follow the instructions on the packet.

This preparation contains a nematode to control vine weevil grubs. It should be mixed with water and the resulting suspension can then be watered onto the soil (see page 14).

Amblyseius species

Two tiny mite species, *A. mackenziei* and *A. cucumeris,* are used to control thrips (thunderflies). Both are pale-brown predatory mites about 1 mm long with slightly flattened pear-shaped bodies, and they eat the immature nymphs of the thrips. *Amblyseius* can survive on other creatures such as spider mites, so once a population has been introduced it may survive even after the thrips have been killed.

These mites are usually sent out mixed with bran. You can sprinkle them around the plants, or else hang the opened containers on the plants and allow the mites to emerge. To help them survive, keep the air humid and the greenhouse well shaded.

Aphidius species

These tiny black parasitic wasps are native to the UK. They are slender, measuring about 2 mm in length, and their larvae develop inside aphids. The wasps each lay a single egg into an immature aphid, then the egg swells and hatches, killing the aphid. The swollen mature aphid is usually metallic brown by this stage, and the *Aphidius* wasp finally emerges from a circular hole in the back of the aphid.

This parasite is usually sent out in the form of adult wasps or parasitised aphids, or a mixture of both.

Aphidoletes aphidomyza

This is the name of a species of midge, the larvae of which eat aphids. The adult midges are slender and about 2 mm long, and feed on the honeydew excreted by the aphids. The orange-red larvae are 0.1 in (3 mm) long; they are maggot-like but taper at both ends.

These predators are usually sent out as pupae mixed with vermiculite, which should be sprinkled at the base of the plant. Because the midges enter a dormant phase if the day length is too short, they are normally only available from April through to September.

Bacillus thuringiensis

This bacterium causes a fatal disease in butterfly and moth caterpillars that have eaten infected leaves. The product that you buy is a dry powder containing crystals of a protein toxic to caterpillars, together with bacterial spores that cause infected caterpillars to die from septicaemia.

The product will kill most types of caterpillar that feed on leaves, including species that you may wish to attract to the garden. But fortunately caterpillars usually feed on specific crops, so spraying your cabbages to protect them against cabbage white butterflies will not affect the peacocks and red admirals, whose caterpillars feed mainly on nettles.

You should mix the powder with water, which you then spray onto the plants. Always bear in mind that rain may reduce its effectiveness, and that new growth will not be protected.

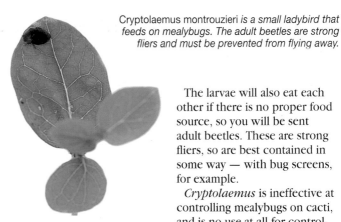

Cryptolaemus montrouzieri is a small ladybird that feeds on mealybugs. The adult beetles are strong fliers and must be prevented from flying away.

Cryptolaemus montrouzieri

This dark-brown to black ladybird came originally from Australia. It is 0.16 in (4 mm) long, with an orange head and rear end. The white larva grows up to 0.4 in (10 mm) in length, and resembles a large mealybug with its waxy covering. Both the adults and their larvae eat adult mealybugs and their eggs. If there are not enough mealybugs, they will also eat young scale insects.

The larvae will also eat each other if there is no proper food source, so you will be sent adult beetles. These are strong fliers, so are best contained in some way — with bug screens, for example.

Cryptolaemus is ineffective at controlling mealybugs on cacti, and is no use at all for controlling root mealybugs, as these are inaccessible to the predator. (See also *Leptomastix dactylopii* on page 15.)

Delphastus pusilis

This tiny black ladybird attacks whitefly at all stages of their life-cycle. Like other ladybirds it's a good flier, so is best confined with a bug screen for a week or two after introduction. Like *Cryptolaemus* this insect is supplied in the form of adult beetles.

Delphastus is not suitable for use outdoors, as it prefers a temperature range of 59-70°F (15-21°C). (See also *Encarsia formosa* overleaf.)

Delphastus pusilis, a tiny ladybird that controls whitefly, is being released from the tube in which it was sent. The paper has been pulled out to encourage the beetles to crawl out onto the leaves of the plant. The tube and paper should be left in contact with the plant until all the insects have emerged.

Most of the whitefly scales on this leaf have turned black — victims of the tiny parasitic wasp Encarsia formosa.

Encarsia formosa

A black-and-yellow parasitic wasp about 1 mm long, which lays it eggs in the scale-like nymphs of whitefly. The con trol is usually supplied in the form of parasitised whitefly scales containing the pupae of *Encarsia* and looking like small black scales.

The adult female *Encarsia formosa* is attracted by the scent of the honeydew excreted by the whitefly, and it lays its eggs in the young whitefly scales. Once parasitised, they turn black after about 10 days — a sure sign that the *Encarsia* is doing its job.

Encarsia should be introduced as soon as you notice any glasshouse whitefly. It requires good light and a warm temperature, and stands the best chance of survival once the warm sunny days of March have arrived.

Releasing Encarsia formosa *to control whitefly*

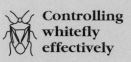

Controlling whitefly effectively

Both *Encarsia formosa* (left) and *Delphastus pusilis* (see previous page) can be used to control whitefly.

Encarsia is generally sufficient on on its own if the whitefly population is low, but you should introduce both predators if there is a medium or severe infestation.

Heterorhabditis megidis

This microscopic eelworm (nematode) kills the vine weevil in its larval stage, though to be effective it requires a soil temperature above 54°F (12°C).

The best time for application to reduce the vine weevil population is in late August or early September, when a high proportion of the weevils are in their larval phase. However, a repeat treatment in May is advisable.

The nematodes should be mixed with water to produce a suspension for watering onto the soil around vulnerable plants (see picture on page 12). The treatment is most effective for pot plants, but outdoor beds and borders can also be treated.

Hypoaspis miles

A species of soil-dwelling mite about 1 mm long that feeds on the larvae of fungus gnats (sciarid flies). Both the adults and larvae are effective predators.

Hypoaspis is likely to be supplied in a mixture of peat and vermiculite, which should be added to the potting compost of vulnerable plants. (See also *Steinernema* below.)

Leptomastix dactylopii

This parasitic wasp lays its eggs in mealybugs, which when parasitised turn brown and swollen, then look 'mummified'. The small wasps then emerge from circular holes.

Leptomastix will only attack certain species of mealybug, and for success it requires temperatures above 77°F (25°C) and plenty of sunlight. It is normally used in conjunction with *Cryptolaemus montrouzieri* (see page 13).

Leptomastix dactylopii is *a tiny parasitic wasp that lays its eggs inside mealybugs.*

Just visible in the central vein of this leaf is the tiny orange mite Phytoseiulus persimilis, *which is used to control red spider mites.*

Metaphycus helvolus

A parasitic wasp about 2 mm long that lays its eggs in soft scale insects — though it only attacks them when they are young. The scale insect is killed as the wasp larva develops inside it. The larva pupates and the adult emerges through a circular hole.

The wasps are supplied as adults, and must be released without delay. Metaphycus is only suitable for soft scale on plants under glass, and requires a temperature of 72°F (22°C) for at least a few hours during the day.

Phasmarhabditis hermaphrodita

This microscopic nematode infects slugs with a fatal disease. The parasites are supplied suspended in clay, which should be mixed with water for application as a soil drench. The nematodes live in the moisture surrounding the soil particles, so the mixture should be applied to moist ground.

Once the nematodes have entered a slug, they will transmit a fatal disease. Large snails will not be killed, but young ones may succumb.

Phytoseiulus persimilis

A predatory mite that eats red spider mites as eggs, nymphs and adults, although it is scarcely larger than the tiny spider mite that it attacks. The adult form is orange-red in colour, with a pear-shaped body and long legs. The immature mites are pale pink and more oval in shape.

Phytoseiulus is a very efficient control, multiplying rapidly when conditions are right. A single mite can eat many hundreds of red spider mites in its life.

The predator must be introduced early during the infestation, and the air temperature should be about 68°F (20°C) with fairly high humidity. Damping down (splashing water on the paths) and misting will help.

Phytoseiulus will not control carnation or cyclamen mites.

Steinernema species

These beneficial microscopic nematodes (eelworms) can be used to control fungus gnats (sciarid flies) and vine weevils.

15

Sex appeal

Pheromones are volatile chemicals given off by some insects as a means of communication. The ones relevant for pest control are those given off by females to attract potential mates.

Chemical lures are available that attract male codling, plum or pea moths into a trap. Commercial growers use the number of males caught to calculate the likely infestation and judge the best time for spraying their fruit crops. But for an amateur gardener with just a few apple or plum trees, catching sufficient males in the trap may be enough to minimise the problem, as without males the females can't lay fertile eggs, so there are fewer maggots.

Traps vary in design, some capturing the offending moths on a sticky surface, while others are filled with a mixture of cooking oil and water. Normally the lure is replaced after five weeks.

Each pheromone is specific to a particular moth species, so there is no risk of luring other moths and butterflies, or beneficial insects such as bees, to their death.

The traps should put out in mid-May to catch codling moths in apple or pear trees, and plum moths in plum trees. One trap for every three trees is sufficient.

They are mixed with water to form a suspension for watering or spraying onto the soil. The eelworms swim around in the moisture surrounding the soil particles, seeking out their prey, and this is why the soil should be moist before application.

Steinernema bibionis is used to control fungus gnats (sciarid flies) by killing their larvae. The eelworm enters the maggot through body openings, and releases a bacterium that lives in its gut, killing the maggot within a couple of

A pheromone trap to lure codling moths is here being placed in an apple tree. The trap gives off a smell that lures male moths in search of a female.

days. (*Hypoaspis miles*, a tiny mite, can also be used to control fungus gnats; see previous page.)

Steinernema carpocapae is a closely related eelworm that infects vine weevil grubs with a fatal disease, in the same way as described for sciarid flies.

Traps and pits

Pea moths can be lured by using the appropriate pheromone as the plants come into flower. You will need one trap for every 65-ft (20-m) row.

Pheromone traps are also available for ordinary wasps. These may help if you find them troublesome, especially in late summer and early autumn.

Buying pheromone traps

Pheromone traps and extra lures are available by mail order, but as they have a longer shelf life than living insects, you may also be able find them in garden centres. Keep unused lures sealed, and ideally in a refrigerator until ready for use.

A saucer filled with beer will serve as a simple slug trap if the rim is just above soil level. Clean it out and top it up regularly.

Trapping is an old and well-tried method of pest control that has recently come back into favour for dealing with various everyday pests such as slugs. In the case of mammal

Doing the necessary

Whether you pick off insects by hand or use traps to catch them alive, then somehow you have to kill them. If you're squeamish this may seem a difficult job, but in fact all you have to do is drop them in a container of soapy water.

pests such as mice and moles, traps never went out of fashion in the first place.

Some people are put off using traps because of the need to dispose of the pests afterwards, but on the credit side they are generally cheap, and harmless to pets and most other animals.

Traps are unlikely to eliminate pests from your garden, but they can help in the short term over limited areas, and are extremely useful as part of an integrated approach to pest control.

Slug traps

You can buy proprietary slug traps, but they are easy to improvise yourself. Simply part-sink a yoghurt pot into the ground, leaving the rim a little above soil level to prevent any earth falling in; then part-fill the pot with beer. Slugs and even snails will be attracted and drown in the liquid.

If you find this visually unacceptable, use a margarine container and cover it with the lid, but remember to cut small holes in the sides to allow access for these beer-loving creatures.

You can also use empty grapefruit halves after the flesh has been eaten or squeezed. Leave them inverted on the soil to create a snug dome under which both slugs and

If you eat a lot of grapefruit or oranges, use the skins to trap pests such as slugs and woodlice before going on to discard them.

Flying insects

Sticky traps are sometimes used to monitor the level of infestation of pests such as whitefly, aphids and thrips, but in a small greenhouse they may actually help to reduce the population, especially if you shake the plants periodically to make whitefly take to the air.

Sticky traps are usually yellow, as this attracts insects — they don't see colour as we do, but they do seem to respond to the light wavelengths that this particular colour emits.

woodlice will take refuge. Prop one edge up slightly on a stone so they gain access easily. Lift them each morning and remove any offending pests. Don't leave the skins for more than a few days, however, as they'll soon start to rot.

Snails

Snails hide themselves in dark places during the heat of day, and if you find their hiding places you will catch dozens of them at a time.

Try leaving some inverted flower pots among the border plants, with one side propped up slightly to allow access. Check the pots each morning, and remove any snails you find hiding there.

Earwigs

An earwig trap is traditionally made from straw stuffed into an inverted plant pot and

supported on a cane among the plants. But if you want something less obtrusive, you could use pieces of rolled-up newspaper left on the soil. Either way you'll have to check the traps regularly and knock out any insects hiding there during the day.

Earwig traps may lack elegance but they can be very effective among vulnerable plants such as dahlias.

Light traps used to be widely used to trap moths, but nowadays these have been largely superseded by pheromone traps (see page 16).

Wasp traps

You can buy pheromone traps to attract wasps (see page 17), but it's simple enough to make your own wasp trap from an old jam-jar.

Half fill it with beer or sugary water, and seal it with paper or a kitchen foil secured with an elastic band. Make a small hole in the paper or foil, just large enough for the wasps to crawl through. They should fall in and drown. (Be prepared to empty and refill the trap periodically.)

Finally, tie some string around the neck of the jar and make a loop to suspend it by. Then hang it in a tree, well away from small children.

Mouse traps

Mice can do considerable damage to stored crops, seeds, and bulbs in the ground. Sown peas and beans are also vulnerable until they germinate. Physical barriers may keep mice away — if not, traps or baits are the best options.

The traditional spring trap is very effective, but you must take great care not to place them where pets, birds and other harmless creatures could trigger them.

Otherwise 'humane' traps may be a better solution, as they pose no risk to pets or

Sticky traps can be used to monitor the numbers of flying insects present, as a guide for spraying, but they may actually catch sufficient of them to help reduce the population. The colour yellow is particularly attractive to insects.

other animals. These traps capture the mice alive, giving you the option of either killing them on the spot or releasing them elsewhere.

Whatever kind of trap you use, always handle it with care and follow the manufacturer's instructions carefully. Handle all materials with gloved hands so that you don't leave your scent on them.

Pits for predators

Ground beetles and rove beetles — those large, fast-moving black beetles so often seen scurrying away when you move things — eat many grubs and harmful insects.

There are various ways of encouraging these predators to stay within a limited area that you particularly want to protect, such as a small bed of valuable plants. You can either

lower the soil level to form a shallow pit, or you can use sheets of metal or plastic lawn-edging to confine the beneficial ground-roving beetles. It's also helpful to provide hiding places for these beetles, such as a tile or slate supported close to the ground on three or four small stones.

This is not, however, a solution in itself, and best regarded as a part of an integrated pest-control system. If you find beneficial beetles in other parts of the garden, you can place them in the bed to be protected.

19

Putting up barriers

Barrier methods can be very effective, and the only drawback is their visual intrusion. Some of them are quite obtrusive — which might not matter in the kitchen garden but may be unacceptable in an ornamental area.

Most barrier methods are fairly cheap to install, though a proper fruit cage to keep out birds can be a costly investment that has to be justified over a number of years. On the other hand, simply draping fleece or an environmental mesh over a few soft fruit bushes such as black- or redcurrants can be just as effective on a small scale.

Keeping out the birds

Bird scarers seldom live up to the claims made for them, as anyone will appreciate who has seen birds perching on a scarecrow — though some kinds are admittedly worth trying (see page 24).

Netting is the surest way to protect ripening fruit, and it can be the best way to protect overwintering leafy crops from the depredations of wood pigeons.

Proprietary fruit cages are the best way to protect a soft fruit garden, and over a number of years the cost will be recouped in terms of the extra fruit available for harvesting. Blackbirds, for example, can strip a redcurrant or gooseberry bush in a day or two, and can make a strawberry crop unharvestable by pecking at the fruit.

If you need to protect just a few soft fruit bushes, then try covering them when the fruits begin to ripen, using either environmental mesh or horticultural fleece.

Mesh size

Fruit cages will not be effective if the mesh size is wrong.

To prevent birds such as bullfinches getting through, use a 0.8-in (20-mm) mesh; it doesn't matter if very small birds such as wrens get through, as these will feed on insects.

To keep wood pigeons and other large birds off winter greens and other vegetables, a 4-in (10-cm) mesh is adequate.

If you only have a few soft fruit bushes, you can achieve sufficient protection by draping horticultural fleece or an environmental mesh over the plants. Mesh or fleece protection may not look attractive, but will only be needed for only a few weeks altogether. Fleece can be reused many times if you are careful not to tear it, while environmental meshes can last for years. It's essential, however, to peg the material down all the way round the bush, or else the more determined birds will find a way in.

Relatively low netting like this may be sufficient to keep rabbits off individual beds, although it will not protect the garden as a whole.

If you have a fruit cage, you should leave the netting off for as long as possible, to allow birds to control the insect pests. Only cover the frame when the fruit buds need protection from birds such as bullfinches, and then later when the ripening fruit comes under threat from the likes of blackbirds and thrushes. Removing the netting in winter also reduces the risk of damage from heavy snowfalls.

If you grow strawberries under polythene tunnels for an early crop, then as the crop ripens you can simply replace the polythene with fleece or fine-mesh netting, using the same hoops.

Home-made dowel or cane frames can be used for the temporary winter protection of vegetables. Special plastic corner pieces are available to make them easy to assemble.

Bear in mind that any frame should hold the net at least 2 in (5 cm) away from the crop, otherwise birds may still cause damage by reaching through.

Rabbits and deer

The best way to deal with rabbits and hares is to fence the garden. Wherever there are hedges or fences of an open construction, make sure there is wire mesh all around with a diameter of 0.7 in (18 mm). The netting doesn't need to be more than 30 in (75 cm) tall, but it must be buried at least 6 in (15 cm) below the ground to avoid rabbits burrowing beneath it.

For deer the fence must be at least 6 ft (1.8 m) high, as they are good jumpers. If the animals are really troublesome, an electric fence of the type used by farmers may be a better solution.

Cloches and fleeces

Cloches are used primarily to warm the soil and offer crops extra warmth early in the season. Afterwards some types can be covered with insect-proof netting or fleece to keep out flying insects and birds. But you need to make sure the plants are healthy first: aphids can thrive within the sheltered environment beneath the fabric, and it may be necessary to spray your crops first.

Sheets of horticultural fleece are often used in kitchen gardens to warm the soil and speed up the germination of vegetables. It's worth leaving the fleece on for as long as possible, as it offers some protection from flying insects such as carrot fly. Remove it for weeding and thinning, but replace it afterwards until the crops become too cramped. Don't forget to check for other pests such as slugs, which otherwise may thrive undisturbed beneath the fleece.

Horticultural fleece and special bug screens are very useful for containing introduced predators in a greenhouse (see page 9). Special insect-proof screens can be bought to fix over greenhouse doors and ventilators. These will not only stop introduced predators flying out but also prevent new pests coming in.

Collars and nets

If you grow brassicas (cabbages and close relatives such as cauliflowers, Brussels sprouts and swedes), cabbage root fly larvae can be a problem pest in some gardens.

A simple barrier around the stem of the young plant will prevent the flies laying their eggs in the soil around the base of the plant. If the eggs

To protect brassicas from cabbage root fly, you can create a simple brassica collar from a piece of old carpet underlay.

are laid *on* the collar, they will either dry out or be eaten by predators before hatching.

Proprietary collars are available, but you can make your own from cardboard or pieces of old carpet underlay. Cut out circles or squares about 4 in (10 cm) across and make a small hole in the middle, just large enough for the stem of the seedling. Then make a single cut from the outside to the centre so that the collar can be slipped around the base of the plant. Firm it into contact with the soil.

Carrot fly frames are easy to make, but they must form a complete barrier all around the bed. You can use a solid barrier or a fine-mesh net that will keep out small insects.

Predators such as ground beetles may shelter beneath the collars, and these will also help to control pests.

Carrot fly barriers

It is the larvae (maggots) of the carrot fly that attack the roots and cause so much damage to this important crop. Although soil insecticides are sometimes used, it's better to stop the flies laying their eggs in the first place.

Fortunately these insects don't fly high above the ground, so a small-mesh screen or sheet of polythene around the edge of the carrot bed will do much to reduce the problem. Make a sturdy frame and fix an environmental or very fine mesh net to it — though you can use polythene instead. Put the barrier in place

before or soon after sowing. The flies are most likely to be attracted when the carrots are thinned, so firm the soil back around the roots, and remove the thinnings.

Slug and snail barriers

Where the visual effect is acceptable, sections of plastic drinks bottles will make reasonably effective barriers for individual plants. You should cut the bottom off the bottle and remove the top to make a mini-cloche for a seedling. For larger plants, you can cut several sections from the middle of the bottle.

Don't assume that slugs and snails won't climb. On the contrary, they will scale a large pot or crawl up a cane. Some gardeners smear petroleum jelly (Vaseline) around the rim

Sticky traps
Sticky surfaces are used in association with a pheromone lure (see page 16).

Grease bands — also a kind of physical barrier — are a traditional method of catching climbing insects such as female winter moths (see page 33 for a full explanation).

of the pots as a deterrent, but this can be very messy.

Slugs and snails are generally reluctant to crawl over rough or irritant surfaces, and traditionally a circle of ash or coarse grit was used around vulnerable plants. Modern proprietary products include crushed volcanic rock, to be applied in a 2-in (5-cm) band around the area to be protected. If you use this method, always keep an eye out to make sure it isn't bridged by soil or foliage.

Such barriers are unlikely to be a complete solution to the problem of pests, but could be useful as part of an integrated pest control system.

Slugs and snails don't like crossing gritty surfaces — which is the reasoning behind this proprietary product that claims to keep them off your flower beds. However, the barrier cannot be effective if it is bridged by soil or leaves.

Repellents and scarers

Chemical repellents and mechanical scarers are sometimes disappointing. Birds soon get used to scarers — they even get to know which cats will give chase and which will ignore them! Chemical repellents are of limited use against cats, though they may help for a very small bed if replenished frequently.

Proprietary chemical cat and dog repellents come in many different forms. This one consists of crystals which you scatter around the plants that need to be protected.

Scarers

There are some devices that do seem to work. Among the most successful are those that detect movement and react by emitting a noise at a frequency that we can't hear but cats can; the detector beam can be adjusted for angle. Other devices detect movement and eject a jet of water as well as giving a visual and audible alarm. These work well because they are triggered every time a bird or animal comes within range and don't simply become part of the background.

Humming lines (special threads that vibrate in the wind) strung across crops can be effective but some birds seem to ignore them. Foil strips which flutter in the wind, fixed to lines above the bed being protected, can be successful — though again their effectiveness may fade with familiarity.

Repellents

These are based on chemicals with a smell that animals find unpleasant or repellent, though they may not be particularly objectionable to us. Irritant substances such as pepper dust are sometimes used to keep animals such as cats off flower beds, but their effectiveness is limited, especially as heavy rain will reduce their potency.

All chemical repellents need to be replenished periodically. It is also advisable to keep changing the *type* of repellent used, so that the animals don't get used to a particular smell and lose their fear of it.

Resistant varieties

The amount of pesticides you use can be reduced if you choose resistant varieties of plants when these are available. Unfortunately, resistance is found in relatively few varieties. Resistant forms are commonest among commercially important crops or popular ornamentals such as roses, where breeders find it worth the effort and expense involved in creating pest- and disease-resistant varieties.

Resistant varieties are especially important if you live in an area where a particular pest or disease is a frequent problem. If antirrhinum rust is rare in your area, then resistance to this disease probably won't be a factor in your choice of which variety to grow, but in areas where it's a severe problem it may be one of the most vital considerations.

Vegetables

Look for varieties resistant to the pests and diseases listed in the table below. The list isn't exhaustive, and new resistant varieties are introduced from time to time, so always check catalogues for further advice.

'Silver Jubilee' roses are resistant to both black spot and mildew (see table overleaf).

Vegetables that are resistant to pests and diseases

Pest/disease	Vegetable	Resistant varieties
carrot fly	carrot	'Flyaway', 'Sytan'
clubroot	kale swede	'Tall Green Curled' 'Marian'
cucumber mosaic virus	aubergine courgette cucumber marrow	'Bonica' 'Defender' 'Petita' 'Tiger Cross'
lettuce root aphid	lettuce	'Avoncrisp', 'Avondefiance', 'Lakeland', 'Sigmaball'
lettuce mosaic virus		'Action', 'Corsair', 'Debby', 'Musette'
parsnip canker	parsnip	'Avonresister'
pea powdery mildew	pea	'Kelvedon Wonder', 'Sugar Gem'
pea wilt		'Greenshaft', 'Kelvedon Wonder', 'Onward'
potato blight	potato	'Cara', 'Estima', 'Maris Peer', 'Pentland Crown', 'Romano'
potato common scab		'Arran Comet', 'Arran Pilot', 'Golden Wonder', 'Maris Peer'
potato dry rot		'Pentland Crown'
tomato mosaic virus	tomato	'Dombello', 'Estrella', 'Shirley'

Resistant fruits

Some fruit varieties show a degree of resistance to the following diseases:

Disease	Resistant varieties
American gooseberry mildew	'Greenfinch', 'Invicta'
Apple powdery mildew	'Blenheim Orange', 'Greensleeves', 'Worcester Pearmain'
Apple scab	'Discovery', 'Gavin', 'Lane's Prince Albert', 'Sunset'
Pear scab	'Catillac', 'Jargonelle'

Resistant ornamentals

Resistance among ornamentals is less common, but in the case of antirrhinums and roses resistant varieties can be of considerable benefit. Try the following:

Disease	Resistant varieties
Antirrhinum rust	'Monarch', 'Royal Carpet', Tahiti Series
Rose black spot and mildew	Varieties showing resistance to one of these diseases will probably have some resistance to the other. There are disease-resistant varieties in most of the major rose groups, so consult a good catalogue before you buy.

Hybrid tea (large-flowered) varieties with good disease resistance include: 'Alexander', 'Blessings', 'Congratulations', 'Freedom', 'Lovely Lady', 'Royal William', 'Silver Jubilee'.

Floribundas (cluster-flowered) with good disease resistance are: 'Allgold', 'Korresia', 'Southampton', 'Sexy Rexy', 'Toprose'.

Among well-tried hybrid teas particularly resistant to mildew are: 'Alec's Red', 'Blessings', 'King's Ransom', 'Peace'.

Black spot is often worse on yellow roses: for a yellow hybrid tea with good resistance try 'King's Ransom'; for a floribunda 'Allgold' or 'Arthur Bell'.

If you want to grow fruit with a minimum of pesticides, then it's a good idea to choose varieties with a proven resistance to disease. 'Sunset' apples, for example, have been shown to be less liable to scab than many other varieties.

There aren't many ornamental plants that have been bred for resistance to diseases. Apart from roses, the notable exceptions are antirrhinums such as 'Royal Carpet' (see below), which are resistant to rust.

Insecticides

All insecticides are intended to kill insects, but the way they are formulated and used affects *how* they kill and how effectively they work.

A few insecticides are very specific in the types of insect they kill, while others are broad-spectrum insecticides that kill a wide range of pests. All these chemicals will be more effective if you use them at the right time and in the right way; the advice here is general rather than specific, so always read the label very carefully and follow the instructions exactly.

Don't forget to check that the chemical you intend using is suitable for the type of plant you wish to spray or dust — and in the case of edible crops, always be particularly strict about the minimum time required after treatment before you can eat them.

Insecticides can be classified according to the form they are used in and the way in which they function.

Contact insecticides

These are insecticides that work through direct contact with the insect, which either absorbs them through the skin or else eats a leaf drenched with the chemical. Sometimes the vapour is also toxic.

Contact insecticides include the following: fenitrothion, malathion, pirimiphos-methyl and pyrethrum.

Contact insecticides have the advantage of being widely available, often relatively inexpensive, and quick-acting.

On the other hand, thorough spraying or dusting is necessary, and because many insects hide beneath the leaves, it's important to apply the chemical to the undersides of leaves as well. This can be a messy business, and there is an increased risk of your inhaling the chemicals, or of spray coming into contact with unprotected skin.

Systemic insecticides

These chemicals are absorbed by the plants and carried around it within the sap. This means that it's less important to wet all parts. Some systemic insecticides are taken up through the roots too, so run-off from the leaves may still be absorbed.

The advantage of systemic insecticides is that the chemical becomes well distributed throughout the plant. This means that sap-sucking insects will be dosed even if they are hidden beneath leaves, or protected by leaves that are rolled or distorted.

On the other hand, the full effect may not be noticed for a day or two after treatment, although some insects will

27

probably be killed when the plant is sprayed. You will need to be especially careful with edible crops, as some systemic insecticides remain in the plant for many weeks.

Sprays

Most sprays leave no disfiguring deposits, and if you use them well a whole plant can be drenched in a short time.

Mixing them can be a trying task, however. It's important to handle concentrated chemicals with great care, and also to achieve the correct dilution rate. The dilution rate may be for larger quantities than you require, and diluted chemicals should not be stored for long periods. They may deteriorate, and it's easy to forget which chemicals are in the sprayer.

Pre-mixed insecticides in small hand sprayers may be more expensive for a given quantity of mixed spray, but they are more convenient and there is less waste.

Suggested chemicals — a guide

Common chemical names have been used throughout this book, rather than trade names, which vary with each manufacturer. The common chemical name is always mentioned as the active ingredient of an insecticide, although it is sometimes given in small print.

The chemicals suggested as controls in this book are not necessarily *all* those which could be used, but are intended to serve as examples. Where more than one is suggested, they are listed alphabetically, and the first ones in a list are not necessarily superior.

Always check the label to make sure the manufacturer recommends the product for the pest or disease you want to control, and check whether the plant you want to treat is on an 'at risk' list (some plants are harmed by certain chemicals).

You should also pay special attention to the manufacturer's advice regarding suitability for edible crops, and always follow recommended minimum times to harvest.

Dusts

Dusts are normally contact insecticides. They are mainly used for soil application and for creating barriers to kill crawling insects. They can be difficult to apply evenly to foliage, especially underneath the leaves, and they generally leave unattractive deposits.

Aerosols and smoke cones

Smoke cones can only be used in enclosed spaces such as greenhouses — and also conservatories, provided there

Products formulated as dusts are usually contact insecticides. Although some are intended for dusting onto leaves, most of them are for application to the soil, to paths or to the routes normally followed by insects to be controlled.

is no risk of the smoke entering your home. The advantage of smoke cones is that they penetrate all parts of the structure, including staging, and nooks and crannies that sprays might otherwise miss.

Aerosols are generally unsuitable for garden use, but are a handy way to apply pesticides in a greenhouse or conservatory, or in the home. Aerosols sold for houseplants normally use formulations that don't have the pungent smell of some outdoor sprays. But you must follow the instructions regarding the minimum

distance for application, as the propellant can scorch the foliage if you hold the can too close to the plant.

Pins and pencils

Insecticidal 'pins' consist of cardboard strips impregnated with the systemic insecticide butoxycarboxim for pushing into the compost. They are ideal for houseplants, as they don't involve chemicals being sprayed indoors. They are systemic, which means the insecticide is absorbed through the roots and will control most sap-sucking insects.

Insecticidal 'pencils' are used for 'drawing' a protective coating of long-lasting insecticide around an area where ants and other crawling insects are to be controlled.

Some plants are particularly prone to pests and diseases — dahlias among them — but such beautiful blooms make them well worth the effort of keeping on top of pests such as aphids, earwigs and snails. Very vulnerable plants like these are worth spraying or treating routinely, or at the very first sign of trouble.

Fungicides

Like insecticides, fungicides can work either systemically (through the plant's sap) or through direct contact with the fungus. However, established pathogenic fungi are difficult to eliminate. Even if the disease can be prevented from spreading further, crop yield will already have been sacrificed, or the ornamental value diminished, because the tissue has probably already been damaged.

Examples of systemic fungicides are thiophanate-methyl and myclobutanil. Contact fungicides include mancozeb and Bordeaux mixture — a traditional fungicide made from a ready-prepared mixture of copper sulphate and hydrated lime.

When to treat

Unlike insecticides, fungicides are best applied *before* you have a problem. Many are intended as preventive treatments, and early spraying will stop the disease becoming established initially.

To do this you first need to know about the diseases that are likely to cause problems with a particular plant, so that you can anticipate when an outbreak is likely.

Many fungal diseases are worse when particular weather conditions have been prevalent over a period of time. Farmers sometimes make decisions about spraying crops such as potatoes against blight when the weather suggests an outbreak is most likely. They can also subscribe to a service which warns them when these conditions are likely and spraying is advisable.

Few amateurs would take their spraying to this extreme. On the other hand, it is probably best to make a point of using a preventive spray if a particular disease has been a problem in the previous year, as the fungus spores are likely to be still in the vicinity.

Using a fungicide at the first sign of a disease outbreak may prevent a minor inconvenience from turning into a major disaster. The procedure is to pick off all the affected parts, and then spray the rest of the plant, together with neighbouring plants.

Cuttings can be dipped into a spray-strength fungicidal solution to reduce the risk of them rotting before they root. Be sure to wear waterproof gloves when you do this.

Be specific

Always check on the label that the fungicide you intend to use is suitable for the particular disease you wish to treat. Many fungicides will treat only a small range of diseases, and may be ineffectual against others.

Fungicides are only likely to be effective against diseases caused by fungi. Those caused by bacteria or viruses will not be helped by a fungicide.

Cut or damaged surfaces of bulbs and corms can be dipped into a sulphur dust to reduce the risk of storage rots.

Watching the weather

Whether you're spraying with a fungicide or an insecticide, you should always water your plants thoroughly first if they are very dry. They can experience even more stress if exposed to oils or solvents in pesticides. Let the foliage dry, then apply the pesticide until it just begins to drip off the leaves.

Dusting is best done when the foliage is wet. In dry weather, mist them first, then dust. This will help the dust to adhere to the foliage.

Sprays, dips or dusts?

Spray formulations are used for foliage and fruit diseases, while dusts arc normally used for storage rots on bulbs, corms and tubers. Tubers can also be dipped into a solution of spray-strength fungicide.

Wettable powders can be used in a liquid suspension for spraying, or sometimes as a dip or drench.

If you know a plant is vulnerable to disease — like this peach that has had peach leaf curl in previous years — then you can spray it as a precautionary measure at the time when an outbreak is likely.

Know your enemy

In the war against pests and diseases, it pays to understand your enemy. Knowing when to strike at a weak point can be the key to controlling them with the minimum of chemicals, expense and effort.

Often, by the time you've noticed the symptoms, it's too late to control the pest or disease that has caused them. But if there has been a recurring problem in previous years it may be possible to make a pre-emptive strike.

Understanding fungal diseases

Spraying is no more than a supplementary aid towards the prevention of disease. It can be helpful if you do it at a vulnerable point in the cycle of the disease. But if you time it wrongly, it's a waste of effort and money.

By the time you have found scabs on apples and pears, for example, the damage has already been done. For that reason some gardeners spray the young fruit to destroy the spores that land on their surface. But it may in fact be better to spray the young foliage some time before the fruit has even set, as the fungus often appears on the leaves before the fruit — it may be washed onto the fruit later.

On the other hand, the spores may have originally come from a fungus growing on dead shoots at the ends of branches. Spraying these won't reach the mycelium (the fungal threads) deep inside the dead tissue, so it may be better to prune out the dead shoots before any spores can be produced. You can then spray as the leaves start expanding, to deal with spores produced from any shoots you may have overlooked.

Bear in mind that weeds can harbour many kinds of fungi that are capable of infecting ornamental crops. So if you pull up and burn (or otherwise dispose of safely) weeds infected with diseases such as leaf spot or mildew, this will help reduce the chance of these diseases being a problem later on.

Although most fungal diseases are specific to one type of plant or family of plants, many weeds are closely enough related to garden plants to pose a potential problem. Such is the case with clubroot, a serious disease of vegetables such as cabbages and swedes. It is difficult to eradicate, and an important part of controlling it is to avoid growing susceptible plants on infected ground. Closely related weeds such as charlock and shepherd's purse may be a source of infection, and these must be eradicated too.

Disposing of problems

Brown rot of apples can be reduced simply by picking up windfalls before they decay and spores are released. Apples that rot on the ground in autumn may be the source of next year's rots, which could affect fruit either on the tree or in store.

Left *Here is a traditional way to control winter moths on apple trees. In autumn or early winter, a special grease is applied in a band all round the trunk, and this stops the flightless adult females in their tracks as they climb the trunk.*

Right *Modern versions of the grease band are much less messy to apply!*

Pre-empting pests

Maggoty apples are probably the result of codling moths laying their eggs in the developing fruit. By the time the maggot decides to make its way out of the apple, the damage has already been done. The most effective control method is to spray with an appropriate insecticide in early summer, with a repeat treatment about three weeks later. But timing is critical, as you must catch the young caterpillars before they have bored into the fruits.

Winter moth caterpillars do their damage to the blossom and developing apples (and other tree fruits) at about the same time, but you should think about control measures as early as the previous winter.

The adult female moths have only tiny wings, so cannot fly. They emerge from their pupae in the soil between late autumn and midwinter, and crawl up the trunk of the tree. Grease bands applied from autumn to winter will catch most of them as they climb, and are a practical way to help control winter moths, leaving fewer of the insects to be controlled if necessary by sprays in spring.

Again, it's too late once you discover the distorted or misshapen fruits that have fallen victim to the caterpillars.

By the time peach leaf curl looks like this, you've left things too late. If you want to prevent the disease ever reaching this stage, then you should cover wall-trained peaches and nectarines with polythene from midwinter until late spring to reduce the risk of spores reaching them, or else use a precautionary spray early in the year.

No hiding place

When a favourite host isn't available a particular insect pest, then many individuals will survive on weeds or even plant debris. So keeping down the weeds, and eliminating hiding places and overwintering homes, will help to control pests and diseases as part of an integrated approach.

Garden hygiene

Slugs, snails and woodlice are just a few of the garden pests that will lurk beneath fallen leaves, old pots and general garden debris, passing the winter in the shelter provided. Hiding places not only attract pests, but also make them invisible to birds and other predators.

Fungal diseases overwinter on discarded twigs and canes, or perhaps on infected leaves that have not been collected. Spores may fall to the ground and overwinter there, ready to start a new cycle of infection when conditions are right the following year. Diseases may also lurk on uncleaned pots and seed trays.

You should therefore always keep the garden tidy, and clear up rubbish and debris. The garden will look much better for it, and you'll probably be helping to make the plants healthier next year.

Safe disposal

Dispose of all dead or diseased plant material in a way that doesn't pose a threat to other vegetation. Don't simply allow it to remain near growing plants. Don't leave dead fruit lying on the ground, and dead-head dying flowers if they begin to rot.

This seed tray has provided a cosy home for lots of snails. You should check all pots and other hiding places regularly and destroy any pests you find.

Left *Never use old pots and seed trays without washing them first. Put a garden disinfectant in the water, and scrub them really clean.*

Right *It's a good idea to expose garden pests to the birds, especially in winter. Here the ground around the base of an apple tree is being loosened to expose pests such as winter moths.*

When you have plant material that you know to be infested with pests or diseases, it's best to burn it, to bury it deep down, or to dispose of it with other household rubbish at a tip. You should only use a compost heap if you are confident that it will reach temperatures high enough to kill the disease organisms. If you build a compost heap incorrectly so that it doesn't heat up sufficiently, it may be a source of problems in future years.

Crop rotation

Rotation is not a practical option for perennials such as shrubs or herbaceous plants that grow in the same piece of ground for many years. But if you grow vegetables, you should practise rotation as part of good plant husbandry.

Rotations are designed to help plants make the best use of available nutrients —different types of crop make different nutritional demands, while some crops even put nutrients back in the soil for other plants to use. Rotation also ensures that your crops remain healthy by preventing a build-up of soil-borne pests and diseases.

The principle of crop rotation is not to grow the same crop on the same piece of ground within a period of four years — or perhaps five years, depending on the rotation method used. The ground is divided into three or four zones, and each year the crops are moved round from zone to zone.

Here, in simplified form, is a typical four-year rotation:

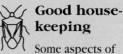

Good house-keeping

Some aspects of pest control are simply a matter of good housekeeping. Keep your garden thoroughly clean and tidy, and lots of pests will never get a chance to establish themselves.

A four-year crop rotation plan

Year 1	Year 2	Year 3	Year 4
Potatoes	Legumes[2]	Brassicas[1]	Root crops
Root crops	Potatoes	Legumes[2]	Brassicas[1]
Brassicas[1]	Root crops	Potatoes	Legumes[2]
Legumes[2]	Brassicas[1]	Root crops	Potatoes

[1] cabbages and their relatives such as Brussels sprouts, calabrese, cauliflower, kale

[2] peas and beans, for example

Identification and control

Pests are much easier to identify than diseases. The majority of them are clearly visible on leaves, flowers or fruits, and are generally large enough to identify. With a few exceptions, they are also easier to control than diseases.

Root pests are the most difficult to identify unless you are prepared to search. Insects that eat the roots may cause the plant to wilt and collapse, or show foliage symptoms that could be mistaken for physiological or nutritional disorders.

Consider root pests if there is no other more obvious explanation. Lift the plant carefully, and shake off the soil to look for pests. Some soil-living pests chew through seedlings or young plants at or just below soil level, so if an otherwise healthy plant seems to have toppled suddenly at soil level, this suggests a soil pest of some kind.

Controlling pests

Most pests are controlled by spraying the foliage, either with a contact insecticide or with a systemic one that is taken in through the plant tissue. Soil pests, on the other hand, are controlled by a soil drench or by a granular insecticide that is sprinkled on the surface.

Biological controls are most suitable for use in greenhouses or conservatories. However, some of those for controlling vine weevils or slugs can be used successfully outdoors if you apply them at the appropriate time.

Identifying the culprit

The descriptions that follow should help you to identify most common pests, and as many as possible have been illustrated.

The different pests are arranged according to the part of the plant most affected, to help you narrow down the possibilities more quickly. But where the symptoms may affect other parts of the plant too, you are referred to other pages that might be worth checking.

Spraying is the most effective way to apply most insecticides. Always check whether you need gloves or other protective clothing, as some are more potentially hazardous than others — and always avoid inhaling the spray.

Roots, bulbs and tubers

Cabbage root fly
Delia radicum
You will notice the symptoms before you see the grub that causes them. Members of the *Brassica* group are affected, such as Brussels sprouts, cauliflowers, cabbages, swedes and turnips. (Radishes are also vulnerable, but being quick-growing are unlikely to suffer so much.) The young plant grows poorly, then wilts.

Pull up the affected plant and inspect the roots. If you find creamy-yellow maggots in the roots or base of the stem close to soil level, they are almost certainly cabbage root fly larvae. In root crops such as turnips, they may burrow into the swollen stem.

This young cabbage has most probably fallen victim to the larvae of the cabbage root fly.

Remedy
Soil insecticides, such as one based on chlorpyrifos with diazinon, will help if applied after sowing or transplanting. Brassica collars (see page 22) are very effective if used around the base of transplanted cabbages, cauliflowers etc.

Carrot fly
Psila rosae
Although carrots are the crop most often affected, this pest will also attack parsnips and parsley, and sometimes celery.

The first signs of infestation are prematurely yellowing leaves, sometimes with a reddish tinge, and stunted growth. If the plants survive this stage, the harvested root will show discoloured orange-brown cracks and lines in the surface, and you may also see yellowish-white maggots up to 0.5 in (12 mm) long in the tunnels produced.

Remedy
The seed rows can be treated with a soil insecticide such as chlorpyrifos with diazinon, but much can be achieved by non-chemical means.

A polythene or insect-proof net at least 2 ft (60 cm) high around the carrot bed will prevent most of the low-flying female flies from penetrating the rows (see page 22). After thinning the crop, always firm the soil around the plants that remain — and don't leave thinnings on the surface, as this will attract the carrot flies.

Chafer grubs
Annuals, vegetables and some bulb plants are the plants most vulnerable to chafers, the larvae of which eat around the base of plants. Young plants

Cabbage root fly larvae are clearly visible on this turnip root.

Beware of the cockchafer — its larvae eat the roots of a wide range of garden plants.

may wilt and die, while root vegetables may have cavities eaten out of them.

The creamy-white grubs have a distinctive C-shape. They are up to 0.7 in (18 mm) long and quite plump, with a brown head and three pairs of legs at the front. They include the larvae of the familiar cockchafer (*Melolontha melolontha*) as well as those of the garden chafer (*Phyllopertha horticola*).

Remedy
These are seldom major pests, and chemical control is only necessary where the chafer grubs are causing considerable damage. Use a soil insecticide such as chlorpyrifos with diazinon. If just a few plants are affected, search for the larvae and destroy them.

Cutworms
These are the caterpillars of several related moth species. Being earth-coloured or creamy-brown, they are often quite difficult to see. They are quite large, however, measuring up to 1.8 in (4.5 cm) long.

Cutworms cause damage by eating the outer tissue at the base of the stem. On a large, vigorous plant this may do no more than restrict growth a little, but young plants may be severed and killed.

Remedy
Cutworms are only worth using chemicals on if they affect a large number of plants (use a soil insecticide such as one based on chlorpyrifos with diazinon). Otherwise you can search them out around damaged plants and destroy them.

Fungus gnat (sciarid fly) larvae
These are mainly a problem of pot plants, especially where a peat-based seed or potting compost has been used.

The adult midges are black and about 0.15 in (4 mm) long, and are often seen jumping over the surface. The white larvae (maggots) up to 0.25 in (6 mm) long have black heads, and may be seen near the surface of the compost. They only attack living tissue if present in large numbers, sometimes chewing off seedlings at the base of the stem or just below the surface.

Remedy
Chemical control is seldom justified, though treating the compost with spray-strength permethrin will work. For a biological control, use the predatory mite *Hypoaspis miles* (see page 15). Yellow sticky traps (see pages 18 and 19) will reduce the populations of adult flies.

Galls
Galls, which are swellings caused by various mites and insects, are normally visible on leaves (see page 44). But the larvae of turnip gall weevils cause swellings at the base of the stem or on the root. At first glance these may be mistaken for clubroot, but if you cut the swelling open you will usually find a grub inside.

At first glance the swellings caused by turnip gall weevils can be easily mistaken for clubroot.

Remedy
Simply remove and destroy all affected plants.

Leatherjackets
The larvae of the well-known crane fly or daddy-long-legs, leatherjackets are greyish-brown legless maggots up to 1.5 in (3.5 cm) long, which feed on the roots of young plants, bulbs and vegetables. Stems may be severed at ground level, and if the roots are eaten, plants may wilt or turn yellow, and possibly die. Leatherjackets are also a common lawn pest (see page 93).

Remedy
In beds and borders it may be sufficient to search around affected plants, pick off the larvae by hand and destroy them. Where leatherjackets are a particular problem, use a soil insecticide such as chlorpyrifos with diazinon.

Narcissus eelworms
Ditylenchus dipsaci
These microscopic nematodes primarily affect daffodils and other narcissi, though bluebells and snowdrops may also be attacked. The eelworms cannot be seen with the naked eye, but if you cut transversely through affected bulbs you will

The stunted, deformed growth of these daffodils is a sure sign of eelworm infestation. The only reliable control is to dig up affected plants together with all susceptible plants growing nearby.

find a distinctive pattern of concentric brown rings.

The first sign that something is wrong is usually stunted and distorted growth above ground level. The bulbs will eventually rot, and the eelworms will readily spread through the soil to neighbouring plants.

Remedy
Chemical controls are not practical, and hot water treatment to kill the eelworms but not the bulbs is not a reliable method for amateurs. Dig up and burn all affected plants, and others within about 1 yd (1 m) of them — and don't replace them with susceptible bulbs for at least two years.

Onion fly
Delia antiqua
Onion fly larvae are white maggots that may be found in the bulbs and roots of onions, causing poor growth and often yellowish leaves. Shallots, leeks and garlic can be affected too.

Remedy
In places where the pest is known to be a problem, use a soil insecticide such as chlorpyrifos with diazinon when sowing or planting. If the pest has already taken a hold, lift and burn all affected plants.

Root aphids
See the section on aphids, starting on the page opposite.

Root mealybugs
These small insects are about 2 mm long and secrete a waxy white powder that often rubs off onto the roots and particles of soil. Pot plants are most likely to be affected; they will lack vigour and may wilt.

Remedy
If just a few isolated plants are affected, it's best to discard the plants and dispose safely of the compost. If many pot plants are affected, it may be worth drenching the potting compost with a solution of spray-strength malathion, though unfortunately this is not always totally effective.

Biological mealybug controls are not suitable for root mealybugs as they cannot penetrate the soil.

Slugs that live mainly below ground cause particular damage to bulbs and tubers.

Slugs
There are many kinds of slugs. Some live above ground or spend most of their time on the soil surface, while others live underground and mainly affect plants with tubers or bulbs.

Remedy
Slugs are very difficult to eliminate, so it may be best to concentrate on parts of the garden where there are vulnerable plants. Baits containing metaldehyde or methiocarb are useful for surface slugs, but those based on aluminium sulphate are a better choice if you are worried about pets or other animals eating the bait.

You can also use a biological control (*Phasmarhabditis hermaphrodita;* see page 15), preferably in spring and autumn. This is especially useful for controlling underground slugs, which may not come into contact with baits.

Traps and barriers (see pages 17 and 23) may be useful for small areas.

Vine weevil larvae
Otiorhynchus sulcatus
Adult vine weevils eat the foliage of a wide range of plants, but the larvae feed on roots underground and can be particularly troublesome. They are whitish with pale-brown heads, and usually have a curved appearance. They cause most damage from late summer to mid-spring.

Affected plants may grow poorly and become stunted, and if badly affected they will wilt and eventually die. If pot plants such as cyclamens or begonias are performing poorly, suspect vine weevil larvae.

Remedy
Insecticides available to amateurs are not very effective. Biological control is a better option, using *Heterorhabditis megidis* or *Steinernema carpocapae* (see pages 14–16). These nematodes (beneficial eelworms) are best watered onto the compost or soil in late summer, when the young grubs are very active.

Wireworms
These slender orange-yellow larvae of the click beetle feed on roots and around the bases of stems. They are especially troublesome when they bore tunnels into root crops such as potatoes. They grow up to 1 in (2.5 cm) long, with three pairs of short legs at the front and a strange 'peg-leg' protuberance at the rear.

Leaf pests

Aphids

These ubiquitous pests are among the most difficult to control without absolute vigilance, and potentially the most harmful. Not only does their sap-sucking weaken the plant; it also distorts or disfigures growth by damaging the emerging shoots and leaves. Also, in the process of feeding, aphids sometimes transmit virus diseases among plants such as dahlias, lilies, roses and tulips.

There are many kinds of aphid, of which blackfly and greenfly are the best-known. There are some species of greenfly that live mainly on specific plants, but this is academic to the gardener, as the consequences and control are similar.

Root aphids live below the surface, so these may not be noticed until the plant wilts or the leaves look sickly, and the control method is different.

Control
Wireworms are seldom a serious enough problem in cultivated ornamental beds and borders, but are a more serious pest of root crops. Where they are a significant problem, use a soil insecticide such as chlorpyrifos with diazinon, or lift the potato tubers early and destroy as many larvae as possible by hand.

Woodlice
These ubiquitous creatures are found in almost every garden, usually hiding beneath rocks or stones, or among rotting wood or vegetation. Also known as pill bugs, they are not insects but crustaceans (i.e. relatives of the crab and the shrimp). They are usually grey but may be pinkish-brown, and have a segmented body that they can roll up into a ball.

Woodlice will sometimes eat living material such as seedlings, but they mainly thrive on decaying matter.

Although often regarded as a pest, woodlice live mainly on decaying plant matter, and are only likely to cause damage to seedlings by nibbling them off at the base.

Remedy
Where woodlice are a nuisance, such as in a greenhouse with seedlings, you can control them with an insecticide for crawling insects, such as bendiocarb; dust it around the edges of the benches, and over other places where they may shelter.

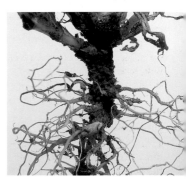

Root aphids, visible here on a viscaria root, often escape notice until the plant begins to collapse.

Greenfly is the best-known aphid, often seen clustered near the growing tips of a wide range of plants. This rose branch is practically carpeted with greenfly.

Aphids are typically green or black, but may be pink, brown or yellow. They are usually about 2 mm long (some species are larger), but the young aphids (nymphs) are smaller. The nymphs shed their skins several times as they grow, and these whitish casts will often be visible along with the insects themselves.

Their complicated life cycle makes it difficult control aphids completely. At some stages they lay eggs (in particular to overwinter the species), but they also give birth to live young — a process the female can manage without the involvement of a male.

Honeysuckle aphids can be a major problem for their host plant in spring and early summer. Later on the winged adult females migrate to live on weeds such as hemlock.

Root aphids (see previous page) are creamy-white to blue-green in colour and about 2 mm long. Wilting leaves are likely to be the first warning that they are present, as they live at the base of the stem or among the roots, often in a large colony. There are various species, affecting crops such as lettuces, French beans and even roses.

Sooty mould (see page 75) often accompanies a heavy aphid infestation, as the fungus responsible lives on the sticky 'honeydew' secreted by aphids.

Remedy

There's no shortage of insecticides that will kill aphids, and prompt treatment at the first sign of infestation can make more difference than the choice of insecticide. Vulnerable plants such as dahlias and roses, and especially plants such as lilies where there's a high risk of virus transmission, are often sprayed routinely from spring through to autumn.

A persistent systemic insecticide is particularly useful for non-edible crops that are vulnerable. Pirimicarb is the insecticide to choose if you want to protect beneficial insects, as it is selective and leaves most of the beneficial insects unharmed. For an organic choice, try one based on pyrethrum or derris, or use an insecticidal soap.

Winter washes with tar oil are a useful way to control overwintering eggs on fruit trees.

Blackfly, here seen on a dahlia, are regular visitors to most gardens. They usually cluster on the tips of young shoots, though you may find them underneath nasturtium leaves.

For a biological solution, see *Aphidius* on page 12.

Root aphids are best controlled by drenching the soil with a spray-strength insecticide such as dimethoate with permethrin, or pirimicarb.

Blackfly
See aphids above.

Capsid bugs
Capsids are pale-green insects about 0.25 in (6 mm) long. The leaves at the tips of the shoots become distorted, and may be peppered with small holes where the bugs have been sucking the sap and have killed some of the cells. Flower petals may also be damaged or distorted. The damage may become visible before the insects, which seldom form large colonies like aphids.

Remedy
As soon as you notice anything, spray with an insecticide such as dimethoate with permethrin or fenitrothion.

Caterpillars
Every child knows what a caterpillar looks like, but there are many kinds belonging to both moths and butterflies, and few of us can identify all of them at a glance. Fortunately, relatively few of them are serious garden

pests, and you don't have to know the species to decide on the method of control.

Most caterpillar pests eat holes in the leaves of crop or ornamental plants, such as cabbages or nasturtiums — in a severe infestation they may even defoliate them. Others are small, often green, and hide themselves by rolling up in a developing leaf or covering themselves in a silk-like webbing. You should open curled leaves and investigate the contents of webbing to see if caterpillars are the cause.

If the caterpillars are few and are not stripping the foliage rapidly, then their droppings may be the first visible clue.

Some caterpillars live on or in the soil, but these are described elsewhere.

Remedy
Caterpillars affecting house or greenhouse plants can usually be controlled by hand picking. This may also be a practical

solution in the garden provided the infestation is not too heavy. If the caterpillars have only recently hatched, they may be massed on relatively few leaves, which you can cut off and destroy.

Where they are present in large numbers, use an insecticide such as derris (rotenone), pyrethrum or carbaryl, and make sure you spray or dust all affected parts. On food crops you may prefer to use the biological control *Bacillus thuringiensis* (see page 13).

Winter moths, which infest fruit trees such as apples and some deciduous shrubs, can also be controlled by using tree (grease) band traps from mid-autumn (see page 33).

Earwigs
Forficula auricularia
These brown insects about 0.7 in (18 mm) long have a distinctively pincer-like rear end. But they are not normally seen

The caterpillars of the large cabbage white butterfly are a widespread pest, attacking ornamentals such as nasturtiums as well as cabbages themselves.

during the day because they feed at night. Earwigs shred the leaves of vulnerable plants such as dahlias and clematis, but are not a serious pest for most ornamentals. They also eat some aphids and codling moth eggs, so are not always a problem in the garden.

Remedy
Earwigs can be controlled by insecticides such as lindane or permethrin (best applied at dusk). It's only worth spraying or dusting plants that are particularly susceptible to the pest. You can also achieve good control among vulnerable plants by trapping the insects with straw stuffed into inverted pots (see page 18).

Earwigs will chew leaves like those of the mallow in this picture, but on most plants the damage is minor. If you want to confirm that earwigs are the culprits, you should go out with a torch at night.

Flea beetles
These small black beetles (some species have a yellow stripe down each wing case) jump when disturbed, but you seldom see them unless you look for them. The first symptoms you are likely to notice are the small holes they puncture in the leaves of brassicas such as cabbages and cauliflowers, and wallflowers among the ornamentals.

Remedy
Seedlings are the most vulnerable plants. Dust the emerging seedlings with an insecticide such as carbaryl, derris (rotenone), lindane or pyrethrum.

Galls
Galls are raised structures, often like blisters or warts, on the leaves of certain plants. They are caused by mites or certain wasps.

Gall mites
These microscopic creatures feed on the foliage or in buds, secreting a chemical that stimulates the host plant into producing a gall.

Gall wasps
These are much smaller than ordinary wasps — usually less than 0.25 in (6 mm) long — and they feed mainly on oaks and roses. The small white larvae stimulate the host to produce galls.

Among the various galls you may encounter are:

- **lime nail gall** (caused by a mite): red to yellowish-green nail-like protuberances on lime tree leaves;

- **plum leaf gall** (caused by a mite): pale-green blisters on the surface of plum leaves, usually near edge;

- **spangle galls** (caused by a particular kind of oak gall wasp): brownish-red circular flat discs;

- **silk button galls** (caused by a different oak gall wasp): brown disks with a depression in the centre.

Remedy
None is usually necessary, as the plant is seldom adversely affected except visually. If you want to control them, all you need do is cut out the affected leaves or shoots.

Greenfly
See aphids (pages 41–42).

Leaf-cutting bees
Megachile species

These bees bear some resemblance to ordinary honey bees, but they cause damage by removing pieces from the margins of leaves, especially on roses. A clean smooth edge is left where the piece has been removed, which is different from the more irregular edge left by caterpillars.

Sections of leaf cut out by a leaf-cutting bee to make its cell

The bee uses these sections of leaf to make a cell, usually in soil or rotten wood, in which to lay an egg. After laying, it fills the cell with nectar and pollen, then caps it with a circular piece of leaf. Leaf-cutting bees sometimes even make such cells in the potting compost in plant pots.

Remedy

Control is seldom necessary. Besides, the bees act as pollinators, so have a useful role in the garden. If, however, they are causing unacceptable damage to foliage, just swat any bees that you find cutting the leaves.

Leaf hoppers

Although not a serious pest, these green or yellow insects may require control. There are several different kinds, growing to about 0.15 in (4 mm) in length when mature. The adult hoppers have a habit of jumping off the leaf when disturbed; the wingless young nymphs are less mobile.

The first sign of trouble may be a pale mottling of the leaves. Roses, pelargoniums and rhododendrons are vulnerable, but the insects can be found on many shrubs, trees, annuals, perennials, fruit and vegetables.

Control

Spray with an insecticide such as dimethoate with permethrin, malathion, permethrin or pyrethrum.

The white patterning on this nasturtium leaf is a clear indication of the tunnelling activities of a leaf miner.

Leaf miners

There are many kinds of leaf miner, including the larvae of certain flies, moths, beetles and sawflies. The name refers to their habit of burrowing and 'mining' within the leaves of various plants.

The symptoms are pronounced and indeed obvious: meandering white, yellowish or brownish lines made within the leaf where the insect has tunnelled. If you hold the leaf up to the light, it may be possible to detect the insect at the end of the tunnel.

Remedy

If just a few leaves are affected, just pick them off and squash the insect or otherwise dispose of the leaves. If there is a serious outbreak, this can be controlled by spraying with an insecticide such as one based on malathion, or dimethoate with permethrin.

Lily beetle
Lilioceris lilii

The adult beetles are very attractive, bright red and large — about 0.25 in (6 mm) long — and often appear in small groups on the leaves of lilies or crown imperials (*Fritillaria imperialis*). Their larvae are repulsive grubs with rounded bodies that they cover with black excrement.

Both adults and larvae eat the foliage of susceptible plants, and the larvae in particular can devastate a plant, including the flowers, within days.

Lily beetles are now common in the southeast of England, but may also be found in other parts of the country.

Remedy

This is a difficult pest to control. If you have just a few vulnerable plants, a good way to keep on top of it is to pick off the adults by hand as soon

The adult lily beetle is a rather attractive pest to look at ...

... but its larvae, which cover themselves with excrement, are as repellent as they are damaging.

as you notice them. Otherwise you can resort to spraying whenever you see the adult insects or the grubs — try bifenthrin, fenitrothion, or heptenophos with permethrin.

Mealybugs

These insects are most troublesome on houseplants and in the greenhouse or conservatory. Cacti are often attacked. These small sap-feeding insects are usually covered by a wax-like white powder and filaments, and may form colonies on both the leaves and the stems (see page 55 for further information).

Remedy

Biological controls are possible, using predators such as *Cryptolaemus montrouzieri* and *Leptomastix dactylopii* (see pages 13 and 15). Otherwise use an insecticide such as malathion (not in the house) or an insecticidal soap (look for one described as containing fatty acids).

Mealy cabbage aphid
See aphids (pages 41–42).

Red spider mites

There are several species of red spider mite, of which the commonest — *Tetranychus urticae* — affects indoor plants, but also outdoor plants in summer.

The mites are very tiny and usually only visible with a hand lens. The most obvious symptoms are yellowing leaves, often mottled, and a silky webbing around the leaves and stems. The mites themselves, which are less than 1 mm long, are either orange-red or yellowish-green, depending on the time of year.

This Fatsia japonica *leaf is showing all the signs of a severe red spider mite infestation. The mites are only just visible in the webbing between the sections of the leaf.*

Remedy

Red spider mites are not easy pests to control with insecticides, and some strains have already developed resistance to some of them.

In a greenhouse or conservatory, or in the home, it's worth trying the biological control *Phytoseiulus persimilis* (see page 15), though it's most effective if introduced early.

Insecticides to try include bifenthrin, dimethoate with permethrin, malathion and insecticidal soaps; spray at least three times at five-day intervals unless otherwise advised on the label.

Rose slugworm

See the section on sawfly larvae that follows.

Sawfly larvae

Although many of these look like caterpillars, they're not the larvae of butterflies or moths, but rather of insects belonging to the order Hymenoptera. The two groups can be distinguished by the number of legs. Both have three pairs of legs at the front near the head, but whereas sawfly larvae have at least seven prolegs (false legs further back), moth and butterfly caterpillars have five or less. Most sawfly larvae are green, but those of the Solomon's seal sawfly are grey.

Sawfly larvae eat the leaves of a wide range of plants. Some eat only a few plant types, while others are less specific. Apple sawfly larvae bore into developing fruits.

The rose slugworm is a kind of sawfly larva that feeds on rose leaves. It often just eats the lower surface, so you have to turn the leaves over in order to find it. Pear and cherry slugworms are also sawfly larvae that graze away the surface of leaves — in this case on pears, plums and ornamental cherries, along with a few other trees and shrubs.

Remedy

Hand picking is often sufficient to control a small outbreak. Otherwise, spray with an insecticide such as fenitrothion, malathion, permethrin or pyrethrum.

Solomon's seal sawfly larvae, here seen on Solomon's seal, are often present in large numbers and can strip a plant within days.

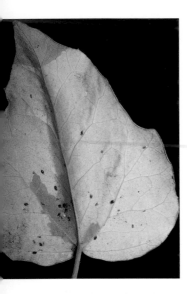

Scale insects
The adult insects resemble scales or small shells, often on the undersides of leaves but sometimes on stems. The young insects (nymphs) are

There are several common types of scale insect that infest both indoor and outdoor plants. These scales are on a leaf from an outdoor ivy.

mobile until they find a place to settle down to feed. There are many kinds, varying in size from 1 mm to 0.25 in (6 mm), but most are small.

Although most scale insects lay their eggs beneath their own bodies, some kinds deposit their eggs among white fibres they have secreted. The young, newly hatched nymphs are the easiest to kill with insecticides.

Among the types of scale you might find in the garden are:

- **cushion scale** (not uncommon on camellias): yellow to brown scales on undersides of leaves; white elongated clusters of eggs;

- **hydrangea scale:** yellowish-brown scales on stems and leaves; white egg masses;

- **hemispherical scale:** dark-brown scales on the stems and leaves of house and greenhouse plants.

Remedy
Spraying is most effective when the nymphs are newly hatched, which is early to mid-summer outdoors, but indoors can be any time of year. Spray with an insecticide such as malathion or pyrethrum.

One of the two main types of greenhouse scale — soft scale, which is oval, flattened and greenish-brown in colour — can be controlled biologically with a parasitic wasp called *Metaphycus helvolus* (see page 15 for more details).

Slugworms
See the section on sawfly larvae on the previous page.

Slugs and snails
These creatures need little introduction. There are many species, most of which are serious garden pests. Most live above ground, but some slugs spend most of their time in the soil attacking the underground parts of plants such as bulbs and potato tubers. Some plants, notably hostas, are

Hostas are susceptible to slug and snail damage, but this plant has suffered a particularly severe attack.

Vine weevils on an outdoor grape-vine — their larvae are especially destructive, but the adult beetles are pests too.

particularly vulnerable, and young seedlings are also at special risk.

Remedy

Slugs and snails are very difficult to eliminate, so you should concentrate on parts of the garden where there are vulnerable plants.

Baits containing metaldehyde or methiocarb are useful, but those based on aluminium sulphate are a better choice if you're worried about the safety of pets or other animals, which could be harmed if they eat the baits. Slug baits are often coloured blue to make them less visible to birds, but placing them beneath plants and under raised stones also reduces the risk.

Biological controls (see page 15) can be used, but are best applied in spring and autumn.

Thrips

Also known as thunderflies, thrips are tiny elongated brownish-black insects measuring up to 2 mm in length Immature thrips are yellowish-orange in colour. Some species have pale banding.

Thrips feed on the upper surface of leaves, causing a silvery-white discoloration, sometimes with black dots. If flowers are attacked, the petals may be speckled, again with silvery-white.

Many kinds of plants can be attacked, but gladioli and honeysuckles are among the commonest victims.

Remedy

Under glass, keep the green-house or conservatory cool and increase the humidity. Spraying with dimethoate with permethrin, malathion, perme-thrin or pyrethrum will usually control these pests.

Vine weevil
Otiorhynchus sulcatus

The grubs of the vine weevil (see page 40) are probably the chief culprits as far as plant losses are concerned, but the adult beetles can also disfigure plants by eating ugly notches out of their leaves.

The adult beetles are about 0.35 in (9 mm) long and dull black in colour, and have antennae bent at an angle about half way along. They come out at night and eat irregular notches from a wide range of shrubs.

Remedy

If you go out with a torch after nightfall, you can sometimes pick off the adult weevils by hand.

The insects are not easy to kill with a spray, but you could try try using bifenthrin or lindane at dusk. Insecticidal dusts can also be helpful if you use them around the base of affected plants.

Otherwise you could try using a biological control to eliminate this troublesome pest at the larval stage (see *Heterorhabditis megidis* and *Steinernema carpocapae* on pages 14-16).

Fruit problems

Apple capsids

Apple capsid bugs can disfigure apples and pears by attacking the young fruit. As the fruits enlarge, the damaged areas develop corky patches and the surface may become distorted or cracked, though the flesh beneath should be sound. The same pest causes distorted leaves (see page 43), especially at the ends of shoots, which frequently have numerous small holes.

The apple capsid is a green sap-sucking bug about 0.25 in (6 mm) long, but you usually notice the damage first rather than the insects themselves.

Whitefly

Whiteflies are like tiny white delta-shaped moths, often rising up in a dust-like cloud when the plant is disturbed. The commonest species attacks house and greenhouse plants, but there are species such as the cabbage whitefly that attack outdoor plants.

Only the adults have wings and look white. The eggs hatch into oval, scale-like nymphs. Older nymphs are thicker and may have a white waxy secretion or hairs on the upper surface.

Remedy

Whitefly is not easy to control with chemicals, but spraying

This branch of Radermacheria stereospermum *is covered with adult whitefly.*

with an insecticide such as permethrin will help. If you prefer an organic pesticide, try pyrethrum or an insecticidal soap. In either case, repeat the treatment at roughly five-day intervals (unless otherwise instructed on the label) until you've controlled the pest.

In a greenhouse, a permethrin smoke cone is a good way to make sure all the plants are treated. In a greenhouse or conservatory, you can also try the biological controls *Delphastus pusilis* and *Encarsia formosa* (see pages 13–14).

Remedy

The flesh is perfectly edible, so you can ignore the problem unless the pest is present in large numbers. Control can usually be achieved (as soon as the petals have fallen) by using a spray containing a suitable insecticide such as fenitrothion, dimethoate with permethrin, or heptenophos with permethrin.

Apple sawfly larvae

The larvae of the apple sawfly cause ribbon-like scars on the surface of apples, before later burrowing into the fruit, where they feed close to the core. Affected apples usually drop off prematurely, and the white maggot with brown head emerges from the fruit in midsummer.

Remedy

Much can be done to control the population simply by picking off any apples with the tell-tale surface scars before they drop off, and certainly before the maggot emerges. Destroying them at this stage will reduce the potential over-wintering population and the chance of a repeat cycle the following year.

If a large population has already built up earlier in the year, then as soon as the petals have fallen you can spray with an insecticide such as feni-trothion or permethrin.

Codling moths
Cydia pomonella

The pale pink grubs of the codling moth bore into devel-oping apples, pears or plums, and feed unmolested in the centre of the fruit. They are usually most active in mid and late summer.

Remedy

Sprays containing bifenthrin, fenitrothion or permethrin are likely to control the pest if used on the fruits in the early summer and again about three weeks later.

If you have just a few trees, then pheromone traps (see

Some codling moths have already been caught in this pheromone trap.

pages 16–17) are useful for reducing the population of male adult moths. The number of insects trapped will also indicate when the females are likely to be laying eggs, and this in turn will help to deter-mine the best time for spray-ing; you must treat the larvae before they enter the fruit.

Plum moths
Cydia funebrana

The larvae of these moths cause similar damage to those of codling moths, but are found in plums rather than apples. The pinkish-white caterpillar has a brown head and feeds inside the fruit, usually close to the stone. The fruits tend to fall prematurely.

Remedy

Spray your trees in the early summer with an insecticide containing bifenthrin, feni-trothion or permethrin.

Raspberry beetle
Byturus tomentosus

We seldom notice the small brown raspberry beetle, but most of us are familiar with its larvae — the brownish-white maggots that live in the ripen-ing fruits. They start by feeding at the stalk end, then move deeper into the fruit. There is often a dried-up patch at the stalk end of the fruit.

The maggots are up to 0.25 in (6 mm) long, and difficult to control unless you time the sprays properly. It's too late once you've started to harvest maggoty fruit.

Although raspberries are the most commonly affected soft fruit, all cane fruits are vulnera-ble, including blackberries, loganberries and tayberries.

Remedy

Spraying must be done before the newly hatched maggots have time to damage the fruit,

so timing is critical. Raspberries should be sprayed when the first fruits have turned pink, whereas loganberries and other hybrid berries should be treated when most of the petals have fallen but before all of them have dropped. Blackberries should be sprayed when the flowers are open. In all cases it is advisable to spray at dusk to reduce the risk of harming bees and other pollinating insects.

Derris (rotenone) and fenitrothion are both suitable insecticides.

Slugs and snails

These familiar pests require no description, though they come in several different forms. The most vulnerable fruits are strawberries, which are readily spoilt as they ripen.

Remedy

If the fruits are being eaten, a biological control (see page 15) is not a practical proposition as a more instant method is required. Gritty barriers (see page 23) are also of limited value around a long row or large bed of strawberries, so it's best to resort to slug baits. If the plants are protected by a polythene tunnel, birds and pets are unlikely to be at risk from the baits.

Wasps

The wasps that are a problem for fruit growers are the familiar social wasps that sting, of which there are several common species. Most people know what a pest they can be in

Snails will go to a lot of trouble to find a tempting strawberry.

the garden, especially in late summer and into autumn.

Wasps can damage soft-skinned fruits such as plums while searching for the soft tissue beneath. Apples and pears are usually at risk when the insects can gain access through an existing wound, such as where a bird has pecked at the flesh. The wasps will eat the flesh, enlarge the hole and provide further access for various diseases.

A plentiful supply of fruit may even encourage wasps to build a nest nearby, which poses a hazard for humans as well as for the fruit.

Remedy

If you know where the wasps' nests are, then you should have them removed. Failing that, you can dust bendiocarb (or some other insecticidal

Flower problems

Individual fruits can be bagged for protection against wasps, but this is only practical on a very small scale.

dust suitable for killing wasps) around the nest entrances — but wait until dusk when the insects have stopped flying.

Traps are of some use (see page 19), but the best protection is to enclose the ripening fruit in muslin, paper bags or horticultural fleece tied around them to exclude access. You could even enclose parts of the branches in old tights, though this is a rather unsightly option and only suitable for the kitchen garden.

Spraying the fruits close to harvesting is inadvisable, especially as the dead wasps will simply be replaced each day as more wasps fly in from surrounding gardens.

Capsid bugs
If the petals develop unevenly, creating a distorted flower, then you can suspect capsid bugs, especially if the foliage looks mottled.

Although many types of flower can be affected, dahlias, chrysanthemums and fuchsias are among those particularly prone to this pest, which is described in more detail on page 43.

Remedy
See page 43.

Earwigs
Forficula auricularia
This very common pest can be a particular problem with full-flowered plants such as dahlias and chrysanthemums, which provide the ideal hiding place for earwigs during the day. But

many other plants can be affected, both annuals and perennials (including shrubs).

Petals that look chewed and shredded suggest earwigs. Check at night with a torch, as that is when they feed.

Remedy
See pages 43–44 for a description of the insect and advice on control.

Lily beetle larvae
Lilioceris lilii
The bright-red adult lily beetles (see page 46) are more likely to eat foliage than flowers, but the larvae, which look like plump maggots covered with ugly black excreta, will feed on

Like other large-flowered plants, dahlias are especially prone to earwig damage.

the flowers once the foliage has been stripped. The petals will become holed and start to look shredded, and the grubs will probably still be present for as long as there is more for them to eat.

Remedy
See page 46 for advice on control.

Pollen beetles
Meligethes species
These small black or bronze-green beetles are about 2 mm long. There are several species that infest flowers, and these may be present in large numbers feeding on the pollen. Pollen beetles are especially prevalent in areas where oil seed rape is grown.

Remedy
It's not really practical to control these pests in the garden, where they cause little damage anyway. But if on the other hand you're cutting flowers for the home, then there is a simple precaution that will remove most of them from the blooms. Stand the cut flowers for a few hours in a shed or garage with a window, though not directly in the window. Most of the insects will fly towards the light, leaving the flowers relatively beetle-free to take indoors.

Slugs and snails
Slugs and snails usually prefer foliage, but both of them will occasionally eat petals. If most

of the petals have been eaten and there are slime trails, then one of these two pests is almost certainly responsible. If you go out at night with a torch, you will probably be able to confirm the culprit.

Remedy
See page 48 for advice on control.

Thrips (thunderflies)
The insects are small elongated black or yellowish-brown flies about 2 mm long. They attack the flowers and foliage of both indoor and outdoor plants, though they are seldom a serious pest.

On flowers, the symptoms are usually a flecked silvery appearance. The foliage may also show a loss of colour.

Remedy
See page 49 for advice on control.

When lily beetle larvae have exhausted the supply of leaves, they will set to work on the flowers. This flower bud has already fallen victim.

Cuckoo spit is the protective coating that surrounds froghopper nymphs, which are also known appropriately as spittlebugs.

Stem problems

Adelgids
These are aphid-like black insects that feed on the sap of conifers, especially larches, pines, silver firs and spruces. Some types cause small galls at the tips of shoots (which they live in); others cover themselves in a waxy white fluffy substance which they secrete.

Remedy
These insects are seldom a serious pest, and spraying a large tree is not practical. If you find them unsightly, try spraying branches within reach with malathion. If you have to reach above head height, be careful to protect yourself from the spray drift.

Aphids
Aphids, especially greenfly and blackfly, cluster along young shoots in preference to leaves, where they can more easily attack the sappy young growth. See pages 41–42 for a description of the commonest types.

Remedy
See page 42 for advice on control.

Cuckoo spit (froghoppers)
Cuckoo spit is the popular name for the frothy, spittle-like mass of bubbles that appears, usually in early summer, on stems and sometimes leaves.

It hides the yellowish-green nymphs of the froghopper.

As the nymphs turn into adult froghoppers, they cease producing the froth and become less noticeable. The adults take their name from their slightly frog-like appearance, having prominent eyes and powerful rear legs, with which they jump when disturbed.

Remedy
The adult insects are rarely a pest worth spraying, and the nymphs are unlikely to cause much damage — though some people find the cuckoo spit unsightly. Try picking off the pests by hand, or spray forcefully with an insecticide suitable for aphids, making sure it penetrates the froth.

Froghoppers
See cuckoo spit above.

Mealybugs
Mealybugs are pinkish-grey sap-sucking insects that are often covered with a white cotton-wool-like substance. They sometimes live on plant stems instead of leaves (see also page 46).

Mealybugs are a common pest of cacti, where they live on the body of the cactus.

Remedy
See page 46 for advice on control.

Mealybugs are a common pest indoors and in the greenhouse, where they live on both the stems and the leaves of plants. Cacti are frequently affected, like the Ferocactus in this picture.

Scale insects

There are many different kinds of scale insect that fix themselves to stems as well as leaves. Among those likely to be found on stems are:

- beech bark scale (resembling a powdery white deposit in the crevices of the bark);

- horse chestnut scale;

- mussel scale (grey to dark brown);

- woolly vine scale.

Remedy

See page 48 for advice on control.

Woolly aphid
Eriosoma lanigerum

The woolly aphid is a common pest of apple trees, including ornamental crab apples. But it can also affect related shrubs such as cotoneasters and pyracanthas.

The most obvious indications of this pest are patches of fluffy white growth protecting the pinkish-brown aphids, which are likely to be found in cracks in the bark or on old pruning wounds.

Remedy

The best time to spray is spring, as heavy infestations later are more difficult to control. Use an insecticide recommended for aphids, such as dimethoate with permethrin, or heptenophos with permethrin.

Of the many commonly seen species of scale insect, there are some that attack a wide range of garden trees and shrubs — in this case a branch of the dogwood Cornus stolonifera.

Below *Cinerarias (Senecio cruenta) are usually only brought into the home for their flowering period. They are very prone to pests such as whitefly and greenfly, so you must always check the plants you buy. Otherwise you could be bringing pests into your home.*

Friend or foe?

Wild mammals and domestic pets can occasionally cause as much devastation to the garden as pests or diseases. Fruits and vegetables are most at risk from birds and wild mammals in search of a meal. But a rabbit or deer can wreak havoc in an ornamental garden, even in a short time. Even our own pets can be a problem, and also a source of irritation to neighbours if they damage their flower beds or spoil their lawn.

Various kinds of barriers can be erected, such as fencing and netting, and these will eliminate some of the problems. But birds and animals can be notoriously difficult to contain or keep out.

Conflict of conscience

Few gardeners have any doubts about the need to control pests and diseases, but we often have to wrestle a little harder with our consciences when faced with the choice of whether to regard wild animals and pets as friends or foes. The fox, for example, is generally regarded as vermin, yet most of us would be pleased to see a fox in the garden — unless of course it was after a pet rabbit or kitten.

Even though we keep rabbits as pets, wild rabbits must be regarded as pests if they arrive uninvited, however appealing they may be to look at.

Dogs can usually be trained, controlled and fenced in or out as necessary.

Cats, on the other hand, are mobile roamers by nature and difficult to confine unless caged. They also have an unfortunate habit of seeking out soft ground to excavate for a toilet — and what better site than a bed of newly sown seeds or young plants? This can be even more of a dilemma if they choose a neighbour's garden rather than that of their owner! You can hardly kill the cat, so the answer must be to deter it in some way.

Not many of us would wish to harm birds either. They can be a pleasure to watch, and some of them are helpful in killing off pests such as slugs. So the usual control method is to keep them away from vulnerable plants.

Cats are good company and kill off the mice — but they also kill birds, dig up our flower beds in the interests of good toilet hygiene, and may sometimes lie down in the middle of our border plants. Keeping pets and a garden can create a conflict of interests!

Dogs and cats

You can protect seed beds with netting or a wire mesh to stop cats digging up the loosened soil. Remove it when the seeds have germinated.

Dogs

Bitches are more likely to pose a problem than dogs, as plants can be damaged when they are urinated upon. Dogs that choose a wall or tree will normally cause little damage, though dwarf conifers and shrubs may become scorched and discoloured. Bitches, on the other hand, often squat on lawns, and without prompt action this will often cause brown patches where grass has been damaged or killed.

Remedy

It may be possible to train your own dog to use an area that won't suffer as a result, and to deter bitches from using the lawn. If your lawn is exposed to other dogs in the neighbourhood, then you might consider installing a low fence or hedge, as this is enough to deter most dogs.

If you notice a bitch urinating on the lawn, or a dog using a vulnerable plant for the same purpose, you should flush the area with water afterwards to dilute the offending liquid. This should be sufficient to prevent further damage.

Cats

Cats will use areas of soil that are easy to scrape as a toilet, so seed beds and newly sown lawns are at special risk, while newly planted bulbs are sometimes dug up during these excavations.

Remedy

There are many traditional ways to deter cats, ranging from orange peel to mothballs, but they are of dubious merit. Pepper dust is sold to deter cats, but its effect will soon be lost after rain.

Some proprietary deterrents are available which produce a smell that is supposed to repel cats. The response to this may depend on the individual animal, but there are certainly some cats that seem totally undeterred.

The most effective methods use modern technology. Some will protect a selected area by producing sound waves inaudible to humans but unpleasant to cats. The beam can be defined in spread and range, so you can even use it to keep your own cats off vulnerable parts of the garden while at the same time affording full access to the cat-flap! Another device can be connected to a water supply so that it squirts water when movement is detected. This is effective against dogs and large birds as well as cats.

Seed beds and newly set-out plants may require only temporary protection, so you may be able to keep cats off by covering the area with wire-netting for a few weeks.

Wild mammals

Deer
These beautiful animals are only a problem in rural areas where gardens back on to land used by them. They are most likely to enter gardens in winter, when they may rub or strip tree bark. At any time of the year they will eat the leaves and shoots of a wide range of herbaceous plants and shrubs (including roses).

Remedy
Repellents and scarers are likely to provide only short-term protection. If deer are a serious problem, a 6-ft (1.8-m) high fence is the best solution. If you use a wire fence the mesh can be large, but if rabbits are also a problem, it's worth using a solid fence or one with a small mesh. Tree guards are useful for protecting the bark of young trees from both deer and rabbits.

Mice, rats and voles
Bulbs and seeds, whether in the garden or in store, are the most at risk from these rodents. There are several species of mice and voles, but you don't need to know which is responsible for the damage in order to control them.

Control
Traps are very efficient, especially if the population is small, but if you use spring traps you must place them where pets, birds and wild animals cannot be harmed. Humane traps designed to catch the animals alive should not pose a threat to other creatures.

If rats are the problem, special rat traps are required.

Poison baits are useful if there is a large population to control, but make sure you place the bait where birds and other animals can't gain access to it, such as under a cloche.

Leaving scraps out for the birds will encourage mice, voles and rats, so try not to put out any more than is eaten during the day.

Moles
See lawn problems on page 93.

This baby wild rabbit is appealing to look at but can do a lot of harm in the garden. Netting is the best way to keep it out of the garden or off your flower beds (see overleaf).

The grey squirrel is regarded as a pest by some — as a charming entertainer by others.

Rabbits and hares

Both these animals are appealing to watch, but cause devastation in the garden, especially in a kitchen garden or among seedlings and young plants. In winter they will also strip bark from young trees.

Remedy

If there's a local population in surrounding fields and hedgerows, or in adjoining large gardens, fencing is the only practical solution. But it should penetrate at least 6 in (15 cm) into the ground — ideally double this — to stop them burrowing underneath it. The height above ground should be about 30 in (75 cm). Wire netting is normally used for this if there's already a hedge, or for an inexpensive barrier bordering a field, but it must have a mesh no wider than about 1 in (2-3 cm) to keep out young rabbits.

Tree guards are useful for protecting the bark of young trees in the winter.

Rats

See mice, rats and voles on the previous page.

Squirrels

Red squirrels are seldom a pest in the garden, and are absent from most parts of the UK.

The more aggressive grey squirrels, however, are widespread and common in gardens. They will dig up bulbs, take berries and fruits, and damage the bark on trees. They will also eat the young shoots on trees and shrubs.

Remedy

The control methods used on woodland estates, such as trapping, are not very practical for the garden. Instead you can protect bulbs with wire netting pegged to the ground — at least until the shoots start to come through. Use fruit cages to protect vulnerable fruit, and protect the stems of vulnerable young trees and shrubs with spiral tree protectors.

Voles

See mice, rats and voles on the previous page.

Birds

Blackbirds
Turdus merula

Blackbirds bring so much pleasure to the garden, and delight with their song, that it seems churlish to regard them as pests. They even assist by eating slugs and many soil pests, and some are great company when you're working in the garden, especially when you're digging.

Unfortunately they are also partial to soft fruit such as currants, gooseberries and strawberries. In some gardens they will strip these crops unless they are properly protected.

Remedy

Rather than attempt to control the bird, you should simply protect the fruit. A fruit cage is the ideal solution if you grow a lot of fruit. Otherwise simply use environmental net or horticultural fleece over individual plants, making sure they are pegged down all round.

Bullfinches
Pyrrhula pyrrhula

These pretty little birds with their black heads and bright-red aprons are mainly a problem in winter and early spring. When food is scarce they will eat buds, systematically working from the top of the shoot to the bottom. As they eat only

Using fruit cages or netting stretched over protective frames is an extremely effective way of keeping birds away from the tempting fruits on offer.

tear flowers and leaves. This phenomenon is not directly connected with feeding, and may be a behavioural activity indulged in at that time of year. In late winter and early spring, sparrows sometimes remove the buds from currant and gooseberry bushes.

Sparrows and other birds can also be a problem with newly sown lawns, feeding on the seeds and taking dust-baths in the soil.

Remedy
Susceptible plants such as crocuses, primroses and polyanthus are sometimes protected by stretching black cotton criss-crossed between sticks pushed into the soil. Netting keeps the birds off but is inappropriate for a flower bed!

Bird scarers may have some limited use on a newly sown lawn, but need to be moved and changed frequently. Recommended sowing rates allow for some loss to birds, so a little feeding on the seed may not be too serious. Some grass seed is treated to make it unpalatable to birds.

The best solution is to sow when the soil is warm and to keep the ground moist. The seeds will then germinate quickly, and birds won't take dust baths in damp soil.

the succulent centres, you may find the outer, harder scales littering the ground beneath the bush.

The problem is made worse by the fact that these birds often go around in small flocks at this time of year.

The fruits most affected are apples, gooseberries, pears and plums. Ornamentals such as flowering cherries, forsythias and lilacs are sometimes stripped of flower buds.

Remedy
A fruit cage is the best solution for fruit, as scarers usually only have a very short-term effect. Alternatively, if bullfinches are a regular problem in your area, you could net individual plants from the end of November.

House sparrows
Passer domesticus
These are only a problem in late winter and spring or early summer, when the birds often

A humming line stretched between canes or supports may help to keep birds off a newly sown lawn or perhaps a vegetable patch. The line vibrates and hums in the wind.

Redwings and fieldfares
Turdus iliacus; T. pilaris
Both these thrush species are winter visitors to the UK. They arrive in large flocks, and can strip cotoneasters, hollies, pyracanthas and crab apples within a couple of days.

Remedy
Scarers can be useful if you move and change them, as the birds will probably be unused to them. Otherwise netting is the only solution, and for trees this is not a practical option. It may be best to make the most of a wonderful sight as a flock of these birds feast themselves and bring their own beauty to the garden.

Wood pigeons
Columba palumbus
These large birds are mainly a risk to the kitchen garden in winter, though they only do a lot of damage during a spell of very bad weather.

They will tear and strip the leaves from cabbages, Brussels sprouts, winter cauliflowers and related crops, and given the chance will eat pea and bean seeds before they germinate. Blackcurrants sometimes attract their attention, and they will strip off many of the buds.

Remedy
The birds will normally get used to scarers after a short time, so netting is the best solution.

Winter pansies, unlike summer pansies, are seldom prone to pests and diseases. The flowers, which start in the autumn, are best in early spring and often larger than those of the same variety grown in summer.

Identification and prevention

The time to act is before a disease can become well established. Here a few leaves showing the early stages of peach leaf curl are being removed. The rest of the plant, which is still healthy at this point, can then be sprayed.

Diseases are more difficult to identify positively than pests, as many fungi and bacteria can only be identified with certainty under the microscope or by using laboratory techniques.

Some diseases to which come under a general label, such as damping off or leaf spots, are each caused by one of several pathogens. But they produce the same symptoms and the treatment is identical in each case, so the exact organism may be of purely academic interest only.

Sometimes the type of plant which the disease attacks gives a useful clue to identification.

Prevention is better than cure

Most diseases live within the plant's tissue, and the first visible clues are either fruiting bodies (of fungi) or damaged tissue. In both cases most of the harm has already been done before a remedy can be applied.

For this reason the best way to control diseases is by taking preventive measures. Coating the foliage, or drenching the soil with a fungicide that kills the spores or hyphae (fungal threads) *before* they penetrate the tissue, is a more effective approach.

Good garden hygiene, with the general aim of eliminating diseased material, will help to reduce the pool of infection for another year.

If you dip all your cuttings in a fungicide before inserting them in the compost (see page 30), this will probably reduce the number of losses due to fungal infection. The same applies to the cut surface of a corm. If you dip it in fungicide this will reduce the chance of fungal diseases becoming established on the wounds.

Damping off, a disease of seedlings, is caused by several different fungi.

Roots, bulbs and tubers

Clubroot
This serious disease affects the Cruciferae (cabbage family) in general, but in particular the *Brassica* group, including vegetables such as cabbages, Brussels sprouts, broccoli (calabrese), cauliflowers and swedes. Wallflowers and stocks are two related ornamental plants that can be affected.

The surface symptoms are poor growth and wilting leaves. If you pull up the plants you will find that the roots are swollen and distorted, and if cut you open the swellings you will not find any insects inside.

This disease is very difficult to eradicate. The spores of the slime mould that causes it can

remain in the ground for many years, and can be carried on tools and boots and on soil moved around the garden.

Remedy
The best ways to limit the spread of the disease are crop rotation (see page 35) and care with garden hygiene — burning all infected plants, and disinfecting tools and boots if necessary. If you don't already have clubroot in your garden, raising your own brassicas is preferable to buying in potentially infected material.

Good drainage and a high pH (plenty of lime in the soil) will help to minimise the effects of the disease, while keeping down susceptible weeds (such as shepherd's purse) will restrict its spread.

If you can't avoid growing brassicas in infected soil, dip the roots of transplanted young plants in a carbendazim or thiophanate-methyl solution before planting. If you're raising the young plants yourself, start them off in a greenhouse and pot them up into individual pots of sterilised potting compost — this will give them a good start when you plant them out, and the crop will be increased even though the disease will not be eliminated.

If your garden is infected, look for vegetable varieties that

show resistance to the disease, such as calabrese 'Trixie' and swede 'Marian'.

Damping off
This disease of seedlings is caused by a variety of fungi. The seedlings die off in patches, collapsing where the stem meets the soil (see the tomato seedlings in the picture below left).

Remedy
As with most fungal diseases, prevention is better than any attempts at control once the visible symptoms are apparent. Sow thinly, using sterilised compost and containers if possible, and avoid overwatering. Watering the compost with a copper-based fungicide will also help.

Foot and root rots
This group of diseases is again caused by various fungi. They attack the roots and the base of the stems of a wide range of plants, but particularly peas and beans, and bedding plants such as petunias.

The roots turn black and soft, and the base of the stem may become soft and black or discoloured (see picture overleaf).

Remedy
You can go a long way towards removing the problem by using crop rotation in the vegetable plot (see page 35), and by never planting the same plant in affected ground for a

Root rots can affect many kinds of plants. Here the two plants on the right are suffering badly from root rot. Those on the left, from the same row, are not yet badly affected.

second year. Remove and burn the affected plants, and dispose of the soil from the immediate area to a place where the disease will not be a problem. It is not possible to save the plants once they are affected.

Fusarium wilt

Although the problem lies in the roots, the first symptoms you notice may be black patches on the stems and leaves, which are sometimes covered with pale-pink or white fluffy fungal growth.

Many kinds of plants are affected, but mainly soft-stemmed plants. China asters and sweet peas are among the ornamentals that are sometimes affected; peas, beans and tomatoes are some of the vulnerable vegetables.

Remedy

Remove all affected plants and burn them. Then try to remove the soil from the area around the affected plant. As the soil remains infected, you should avoid growing the same type of vulnerable plant in the same soil for several years.

Where resistant varieties are available — with tomatoes for instance — you should always choose these if the disease has been a regular problem.

Honey fungus

This is a serious disease of woody plants such as privets and rhododendrons. It normally affects trees, shrubs and climbers, though there have been instances of herbaceous perennials being affected. Many of the conifers used for hedges are vulnerable. It is caused by a specific fungus called *Armillaria*.

Although a root problem, the disease affects the whole plant. You may first be alerted by poor growth and a clear indication that the plant is dying. When the disease is advanced, fruiting bodies like honey-coloured toadstools may appear close to the base of the plant in autumn. Creamy-white fungal threads may be visible under the bark at the base of the plant, sometimes extending up the stem. Tough black 'bootlace' rhizomorphs (fungal strands) may also be found. If conifers are infected, resin may ooze from around the base of the trunk.

Remedy

This is a difficult disease to control, but action must be taken as soon as possible. You should dig up and remove the infected plant if possible. Chemical controls are of limited use in controlling a badly affected plant, but they may help in preventing the spread of the disease to neighbouring plants.

If possible replant with something less susceptible. Examples of shrubs that show good resistance are bamboos, beech, box, *Chaenomeles*, *Cotinus*, *Hebe*, *Rhus*, *Romneya* and yews.

Pansy sickness

If pansies or violets appear to wilt and then collapse, with no sign of insects eating the roots, then they are probably suffering from pansy sickness. This is especially likely if a number of plants die in close proximity to each other on ground where pansies have been grown previously.

Pansy sickness is a fungal infection of the roots that causes the plants to collapse.

Various species of *Phytophthora* fungus affect the roots and cause them to die, though fine roots may remain healthy. Wet or waterlogged soil makes the disease more likely.

Areas of dead leaves or needles may be the first sign, and later dieback may occur over the whole stem. If you remove the bark close to the base of the main stem, you

Various soil-born fungi affect the roots, and the stem may rot at ground level, but the first visible sign may be when the leaves become discoloured and start to wilt.

Remedy
Dig up affected plants and burn them. The fungi responsible can remain in the soil for a long time as sclerotia (resting bodies), so don't replant pansies or violas in the same ground.

Phytophthora root rots
This is a disease of trees, shrubs and other woody plants such as heathers and raspberries. Conifers such as *Taxus baccata* (common yew) and *Chamaecyparis lawsoniana* (Lawson cypress) are particularly vulnerable.

The dieback in this conifer is a sign that the roots have fallen victim to a Phytophthora *infection.*

may see a blackish-brown or reddish discoloration.

Remedy
There are no practical chemical options for use in the garden. The only control for *Phytophthora* root rot is to dig up and burn the affected plants.

Potato blight
Potato blight first affects the foliage (see page 72), but spores washed into the soil may later cause problems on the tubers. The disease causes dark sunken areas to appear on the tuber, together with reddish-brown staining of the flesh beneath. Other diseases and rots readily enter through the wounds, and the tubers cannot be stored.

Remedy
See page 72 for control of the initial infection.

Potato scab
Common scab makes potatoes look unsightly, with raised scabby patches on the skin. The disease is caused by a bacterium-like organism that produces mycelium in a similar fashion to fungi.

Remedy
As the tubers are usually still edible, it's sufficient to reduce the incidence of the disease by cultural methods. Potato scab is more likely in dry summers and is encouraged by light, sandy soils with a high pH (lime content). So you should avoid liming and add plenty of

humus-forming material to the soil, such as garden compost or rotted manure. Keep the plants well watered.

If scab is normally a problem in your garden, choose resistant varieties such as 'Arran Comet', 'Golden Wonder', 'King Edward' or 'Maris Peer'.

Storage rots
A range of fungi cause storage rots among bulbs, corms and tubers. Moulds may be visible on the outer skin, or there may be deeper sunken patches near the surface. When the rot is advanced, a bulb or corm will feel soft to the touch, and the base may be completely rotten. Secondary rots and infections may enter once the tissue has become diseased.

Remedy
Never plant bulbs that look mouldy or feel soft. After lifting

bulbs you should only store the healthy ones — and before storing them you should dust them with sulphur, or dip them into a fungicidal solution and allow to dry. Always store in a cool, well-ventilated place, and check periodically to remove any that are developing storage rots.

Verticillium wilt
There are several species of *Verticillium* fungus that cause wilt diseases. When a plant is infected, the roots die and cause the whole plant to wilt and collapse. When the affected root or stem is cut lengthways, brown stripes may be visible in the vascular tissue. Many types of plant may be affected.

Control
Dig up and burn all affected plants.

Leaf problems

American gooseberry mildew

A white powdery-looking coating on gooseberry leaves and fruit is almost certain to be due to this disease.

See page 78 for a more detailed description, together with advice on control.

Black spot

See leaf spots on page 71.

Botrytis (grey mould)

This ubiquitous disease is ready to seize hold whenever plants are in poor health, wounded or growing in damp conditions with poor air circulation — or simply where dead or dying flowers or leaves are left to rot on the plant.

One reason why the disease is so widespread is that it survives on both live and dead tissue. Also it is not dependent on a particular type of plant: annuals, bulbs, herbaceous plants, even trees and shrubs can be affected, while strawberry fruits are notoriously susceptible (see page 78).

The fungus usually responsible is *Botrytis cinerea*, and the

American gooseberry mildew is a disfiguring disease that commonly attacks this fruit. Both leaves and fruit are affected.

common name grey mould describes the visual appearance once the disease is well established. The grey, fluffy mould contains the spores, which often rise in a cloud when disturbed. In the early stages of the disease, which often enters through wounds, the leaves may turn brown or look discoloured, becoming soft, and later covered with grey fluffy growth.

For related fruit and flower symptoms see pages 78 and 81.

Remedy

As there are almost always spores in the air, it is difficult to eliminate this disease, but good garden hygiene will help — simply removing and destroying all affected parts of the plant. Cut back into healthy tissue, and if possible protect the wound by spraying or dusting with a fungicide such as carbendazim.

Chocolate spot is a fungal infection of broad beans, but is seldom serious enough to require aggressive treatment.

Chocolate spot

This disease is caused by the fungus *Botrytis fabae*. It produces brown spots on the leaves of broad beans, and sometimes on stems and pods too. It mainly occurs in spring, and is worst in wet weather.

If symptoms are severe it may kill the plant, but a mild outbreak will do no more than reduce the yield.

Remedy

Carbendazim may help if you spray the plants as soon as you notice the first spots. Otherwise pick off affected leaves and use cultural methods to reduce the risk of the disease the following year. Grow the beans on well-drained soil, and be careful not to feed them with a high-nitrogen fertiliser. Slightly wider than normal spacing might help if winter and spring are both wet. If chocolate spot is a regular problem, you could also spray your plants with an appropriate fungicide before it becomes established on them.

Downy mildew

This is less common than powdery mildew (page 73), but it also affects a wide range of plants — mainly annuals and border perennials. Among the vegetables, lettuces are particularly vulnerable, though onions, spinach and peas may also succumb to various forms of the disease.

Several fungi are responsible for the condition known as downy mildew, but they all cause similar symptoms. The upper surface of affected leaves usually has brown or yellow blotches, while the undersides usually develop a white mealy growth that sometimes looks fuzzy. In severe cases a whole leaf may become discoloured and die.

Remedy
Remove affected leaves to reduce the chance of the disease spreading, then spray with a suitable fungicide such

as mancozeb. Bear in mind that fungicides for powdery mildew may not be the best choice for downy mildew. Avoid watering from overhead, as a damp atmosphere may encourage the disease.

In future, try to ensure that your plants are well spaced, with plenty of air circulating between them.

Fireblight

This serious disease affects mainly apple and pear trees, but cotoneasters, hawthorns and some *Sorbus* species may also succumb. It is caused by a bacterium, so cannot be controlled by sprays.

The first symptoms are often when the flowers turn black and wither, but the disease isn't usually noticed until the leaves shrivel and turn black (or yellow in the case of hawthorns and some other plants), giving the affected part of the tree or bush a burnt or scorched appearance. Eventually oozing cankers appear on the branches, and by this stage the disease is easily spread to healthy plants.

Fireblight used to be a notifiable disease throughout the UK, and government inspectors would have to confirm its presence and advise on an appropriate course of action.

This pear tree has succumbed to fireblight — a serious disease that normally attacks apples and pears, though it sometimes affects shrubs such as pyracanthas.

This is no longer the case in mainland Britain, but fireblight is still notifiable in the Channel Islands, the Isle of Man and Northern Island.

Remedy
Prune out affected branches as soon as you notice the disease, cutting back into healthy wood by at least 2 ft (60 cm) so that you can be sure of removing all affected tissue. Disinfect the saw afterwards and burn all the prunings. If a plant is badly affected, it's best to dig it up and burn it.

Fusarium wilt

This is a root problem, but the first symptoms may be black patches on the leaves and stems, which sometimes become covered with pale-pink or white fluffy fungal growth. See page 66 for further information and advice on control.

Leaf spots

A range of different fungi and bacteria cause leaf spots on a wide range of plants, but most symptoms are similar and you don't always have to know the exact pathogen responsible to decide on a course of action. Descriptions and controls for the two main categories of leaf spot are set out below:

Bacterial leaf spots
These affect most types of plant, although the organism responsible may vary. Black spots of various sizes, often with a yellow edge or halo and irregular in shape, are typical

symptoms. Unlike with fungal leaf spots, there are no signs of fruiting bodies associated with bacterial leaf spots.

Bacterial leaf spots may be unsightly to look at, but they seldom cause the plant any permanent harm.

Remedy
Spraying will not help. Remove affected leaves by hand, and avoid overhead watering, as the disease can be spread when water droplets fall on affected leaves.

Fungal leaf spots
These also affect a wide range of plants, both woody and soft such as annuals and vegetables. Various fungi are responsible. The best-known fungal leaf spot is rose blackspot (see picture overleaf).

The symptoms are more or less circular black, brown or grey spots (the colour usually depends on the type of leaf spot). They start small but often coalesce to form larger blotches less regular in shape. Close investigation with a hand lens may reveal small black fruiting bodies on the affected areas — these release the spores that can cause fresh infections. In severe attacks the leaves will fall prematurely.

Remedy
Pick up and burn any infected leaves that fall, to reduce the number of spores that survive to reinfect healthy leaves.

Copper-based fungicides are suitable for a wide range of

Black-spot of roses is perhaps the best-known of the different types of leaf spot, and is certainly one of the most troublesome.

fungal leaf spots. Carbendazim and mancozeb (among others) are suitable for some fungal leaf spots, but you should always check the label on the product for a list of leaf spots likely to be controlled.

In the case of roses, if you live in an area where black-spot is common, you should try to choose resistant varieties. Some examples of these are given on page 26, but it's best to consult specialist rose catalogues for the latest advice on the resistance of different rose varieties.

Pansy sickness

Pansies and violas that appear to wilt and collapse for no apparent reason may be suffering from the root infection known as pansy sickness (see page 66).

Peach leaf curl

This is one of the easiest diseases to identify as the symptoms are so distinctive (see picture on page 33). It is found only on peaches, nectarines and almonds, and occasionally on related ornamental *Prunus* species. The leaves become distorted as if with blisters, and then the affected areas turn red. White fungal growth may also be visible on the leaf.

The leaves will probably fall eventually, but new ones may be produced even in the same season. These may be healthy

but could also be affected if they are not sprayed.

Remedy

If just a few leaves are affected, pick them off and burn them as soon as you notice them. You can also prevent infection in the first place by using a copper-based fungicide in mid or late winter, repeating the treatment 14 days later. If new leaves are produced after the leaves have dropped, it's worth spraying these too if there is any sign of the disease returning. A precautionary spray just before the leaves fall in autumn is a good idea.

Wall-trained peaches and nectarines can be protected from the air-borne spores during the vulnerable period (from midwinter to early spring) by making a wooden frame and covering the plants with a clear polythene screen. The screen should be open-sided to keep the plant cool, and the polythene should be removed in late spring.

Potato/tomato blight

This serious disease of potatoes also affects tomatoes, though seldom when they are grown under glass. Affected leaves turn brown, often starting at the tips and around the edges, then rapidly shrivel. In humid weather a white fungal growth may be visible at the edges of the brown areas, especially on the under-surface of the leaf.

This disease is especially serious for potatoes, and the tubers may become infected from spores washed down in to the soil. (See page 68 for symptoms on the tubers.)

On tomatoes, the fruit may have a brown discoloration, and will often rot on the plant or soon after being picked.

Remedy

Spray with mancozeb or a copper-based fungicide as soon as the blight is found anywhere in the area. If the season is wet, it's worth spray-ing potatoes as a precaution anyway.

Outbreaks are most likely if there have been two 24-hour periods when the temperature has remained at or above 50° F (10°C) with a relative humidity of at least 89%. If you can monitor both temperature and humidity, you will have a good indication of when spraying is especially worthwhile.

Earthing the tubers up deeply will reduce the chances of them becoming infected.

There are potato varieties that show some resistance to the disease, including 'Cara', 'Maris Peer', 'Pentland Crown', 'Romano' and 'Wilja'.

Powdery mildew on Michaelmas daisies — a plant that is particularly susceptible to the disease.

Powdery mildew

One of the most common diseases, powdery mildew attacks many kinds of plants, including trees and shrubs as well as the more commonly affected annuals and border perennials. Some fruit and vegetables are also affected. Several fungi are responsible, but the symptoms and treat-ment are similar.

Usually the upper surface of affected leaves is covered with a white fungal growth that normally looks white and powdery (on some shrubs it can be felty and buff-coloured or brown); the lower surface can also be affected.

Remedy

Plants under stress, especially on dry soil, are more vulnera-ble to the disease, particularly if the air around the leaves is humid. Watering and mulch-ing, and keeping the plants well fed, will help them resist the disease. When watering, try to water to the soil without wetting the leaves. Removing affected leaves as soon as you notice them may be enough to arrest the outbreak. Otherwise spray with a fungicide such as carbendazim, mancozeb, or triforine with bupirimate.

Annuals and biennials such as forget-me-nots and pansies sometimes succumb to pow-dery mildew, but if they've already had a long period of flowering, it's best to pull them up and burn them, rather than spraying plants that will soon be removed anyway.

Some rose varieties have shown good resistance to rose powdery mildew, so take this into account when choosing a variety. Rose catalogues usually give an indication of disease resistance.

Rusts

Rust symptoms may be due to any one of a range of fungi. Some are specific to one type of plant, such as antirrhinums, hollyhocks or roses, but a large number of different plants, ranging from annuals and bulbs to border perennials, trees and shrubs, are vulnerable to rust fungi.

Typically, rusts look like small rust-coloured, orange, brown or beige patches or pustules on the lower surface of the leaves. The upper surface above them may be yellow or discoloured.

Badly affected leaves eventually fall off prematurely, and the plant is weakened, sometimes to the point of death.

Rust is often worst in wet seasons.

Remedy

Pick off and burn as many affected leaves as possible, then spray with a suitable fungicide such as mancozeb, bupirimate with triforine, myclobutanil or penconazole. Not all fungicides are effective against rust, and some are suitable for use only on certain plants, so you should always check the label.

Scab

This is primarily a disease affecting fruit, though ornamental crab apples and pyracanthas can also be affected. Scab can be caused by several fungi. Leaf symptoms include brownish or grey patches that

look blistered or scabby, and the foliage often falls prematurely. See page 79 for symptoms on the actual fruit.

Control

Pick off isolated leaves that are affected, or prune out badly affected shoots, then spray

Rust diseases affect a vast range of different plants — in this case a specimen of Oxalis.

As the holes in the leaves indicate, this plant has fallen victim to shot-hole disease.

with a fungicide such as carbendazim or triforine with bupirimate. Rake up and burn fallen leaves and fruits.

If the branches are very congested, thin them out when dormant to produce a more open plant.

Shothole

As the common name of this disease suggests, the symptoms are shot-like holes in the leaves. They start as discoloured spots, which are usually brown, but eventually the dead tissue falls away, leaving a hole.

The disease can be caused by several different fungi and bacteria. Many plants are affected, but predominantly trees and shrubs, including cherries and plums.

Remedy

Treatment is seldom necessary, though the disease can be disfiguring. If necessary, spray with a copper-based fungicide. But it may be just as effective to ensure your plants are healthy and well fed, and thus more resistant to infection.

Silver leaf

This serious disease, caused by a fungus, affects trees, and in particular those belonging to the Rosaceae (rose family); cherries and plums are especially susceptible.

The name silver leaf give a clue to the symptoms: the leaves develop a silvery-grey sheen, perhaps starting on one

branch but spreading as the disease becomes more established. Some branches may eventually die.

If you cut through an affected shoot, you will notice a brown staining of the central wood. This will confirm the diagnosis, but make sure the stem is at least 1 in (2.5 cm) across.

Remedy

Cut out all affected branches, making sure you cut back into healthy wood — at least 6 in (15 cm) beyond any sign of stained wood. Then burn the prunings. Use a wound paint to protect the wound.

Whenever possible, susceptible plants should be pruned in summer, when they are less likely to become infected through the wounds.

Smuts

This uncommon problem is caused by various fungi, and is most likely to affect anemones, dahlias, *Trollius* and winter aconites (*Eranthis*). Oval or

round greenish-white swellings may be visible on the leaves or stems, which then rupture to expose a mass of black spores.

Remedy

Don't attempt to spray — lift and burn all affected plants to reduce the risk of reinfection.

Sooty mould

The name describes the spots of black or grey mould that live on the honeydew excreted by aphids and other sap-sucking insects. It is not a parasitic fungus, so does not directly harm the plant. But it looks unsightly, and if much of the leaf surface is covered it will affect the vigour of the plant by cutting out light.

Remedy

As the fungus lives on the honeydew and not the plant, it can be controlled by spraying the insect pests that created the initial problem. Such pests may include aphids, mealybugs and whitefly.

Sooty mould lives on the honeydew secreted by sap-sucking insects, and doesn't live directly on the plant tissue. Nevertheless it is very disfiguring.

This tulips shows clear symptoms of tulip fire — a serious fungal disease of tulips. The best solution is to lift and burn all affected plants, and not to plant tulips in the same ground for at least two years.

Tulip fire

If the leaves and shoots of tulips are stunted or distorted, and spotted or streaked pale brown, then you should suspect a fungal disease known as tulip fire. Flower buds may develop but fail to open. If there are also grey fungal growths with black sclerotia (resting bodies), the diagnosis is almost certain. The bulbs of affected plants may have sunken lesions, and black sclerotia are often visible.

Remedy

Lift and burn affected plants, and don't replant tulips in the same ground for two years at the very least.

As a precaution with the remaining bulbs, lift them when the foliage has died back, discard any with sclerotia, and dip the remaining healthy bulbs in a fungicide such as carbendazim, or dust them with sulphur before storing.

Verticillium wilt

This disease of the roots causes the whole plant to wilt and collapse, and it may be problems with the leaves and stems that first indicate a problem. See page 68 for a further description together with advice on control.

Tomato blight

See potato blight on page 72.

Tomato leaf mould

This fungal disease is only likely to affect tomatoes under glass. Tomato leaf mould becomes visible as purplish-grey patches on the lower leaf surfaces, and yellow blotches above, starting with the lower and older leaves. The leaves eventually wither and die, but tend to hang rather than dropping off.

Remedy

Pick off affected leaves and increase ventilation. If the disease occurs early in the season, spray with a fungicide such as carbendazim or mancozeb. If the leaves are affected near the end of the season it isn't worth spraying, but it's advisable to lift and burn the plants when they've finished cropping.

Some tomatoes show resistance to the disease, including 'Dombello', 'Estrella', and 'Shirley'.

Suspect a virus disease if just an isolated plant looks distorted or mottled — like the pansy at the front in this picture — while all similar plants around are healthy.

Viruses

Virus infections manifest themselves in many different ways, and the exact symptoms will vary according to the disease. Suspect a virus if a problem can't be attributed to insects or normal diseases caused by fungi or bacteria, and especially if just isolated plants are affected among others that are healthy.

Foliage is likely to be streaked or mottled, often with yellow areas (but make sure this is not due to a nutritional deficiency), and the leaves may be distorted or smaller than usual. Flowers too may be streaked or splashed with another colour.

Growth is often stunted or distorted, whether or not the leaves look abnormal.

Remedy

No controls are generally available to ordinary gardeners. All you can do is lift and burn affected plants.

Only commercial propagation laboratories have the direct means of dealing with viruses, by taking microscopic cuttings from the very tips of plant stems, the cells of which don't yet contain the virus.

Among the major sources of virus infections are sap-sucking insects such as aphids and whitefly, so controlling these pests is the most practical method of preventive action you can take. This is especially important where a large number of vulnerable plants, such as dahlias and lilies, are being grown close together.

Viruses can be transmitted from one plant to another on secateurs and pruning knives, so you should clean your tools extra thoroughly after using them on infected plants.

Wilt

A number of fungi cause plants to collapse. Sometimes the initial symptoms are wilting; sometimes the first sign is brown, almost scorched-looking leaves (as if too dry), followed by a general collapse of the plant. This doesn't necessarily happen rapidly, and on woody plants the disease may start on one part and then spread gradually.

There are wilts of particular plants, such as clematis wilt, but the more general wilts caused by *Fusarium* and *Verticillium* species are widespread among many different plants.

Remedy

See pages 66 and 68, where *Fusarium* and *Verticillium* wilts are described in more detail. For clematis wilt see page 81.

Fruit problems

American gooseberry mildew

This is a common disease of gooseberries, but it occasionally attacks blackcurrants too. A white powdery fungal growth develops rapidly on the upper surface of leaves, and on the stems and developing fruits. The ripening fruit have discoloured patches on the skin, which look unattractive even though the fruit is still edible.

Remedy

If you wish to avoid spraying, you can achieve a lot by cultural methods. Prune plants when dormant to maintain an open bush and allow plenty of air to circulate; avoid high-nitrogen fertilisers that might cause sappy growth. If just a few shoots are affected, prune them out as soon as you notice them.

If the disease is a regular problem, it may be helpful to grow varieties with a natural resistance to the disease. Among those showing some resistance are 'Greenfinch', 'Invicta' and 'Lancashire Lad'.

Once a plant is badly affected, however, a fungicide such as bupirimate with triforine,

carbendazim, or a copper-based fungicide, should help, but you should spray as soon as the disease is visible.

Botrytis (grey mould)

The fungus that causes grey mould — *Botrytis cinerea* — is very common, living on dead material as well as living tissue on a wide range of plants

In the fruit garden strawberries are most at risk, though raspberries are also affected. In a wet season, the developing fruits begin to rot on the plants as grey mould becomes established. The fruits quickly become soft and covered with a fluffy grey growth, which if disturbed may release a cloud of spores into the air.

On tomato plants, unripe fruits may develop 'ghost spots' (pale watery-looking spots) on the skin caused by grey mould. Fruit that is only mildly affected can be eaten, but sometimes the fruit rots as it ripens.

Remedy

Remove and destroy diseased fruit as soon as you notice it. Covering the rows of strawberries with cloches will help to keep the plants dry and should reduce the infection. Otherwise, in a wet season it may be necessary to spray with a suitable fungicide such as carbendazim.

Brown rot

This disease causes soft areas in fruits such as apples and pears, peaches, nectarines, and plums, where characteristic

In the early stages, American gooseberry mildew looks like a white, powdery deposit on the leaves and fruit. But as the fruit matures it develops browner patches, sometimes edged white.

Grapes are among the fruits most susceptible to powdery mildew, which indeed can ruin a crop.

concentric rings of pale-brown or creamy-white pustules appear on the surface. The fruits usually drop prematurely, or else shrivel and remain on the tree. Infection usually enters through wounds created by insect pests.

Remedy
Pick up and burn affected fruits to reduce the number of spores released. This will not cut down the current year's losses, but might help reduce the problem in the following year. You can also reduce the likelihood of infection by controlling pests such as codling moths that damage the fruit.

Powdery mildew
Powdery mildews are common on the foliage of many plants, but among the fruits, grapes are particular susceptible. Vine powdery mildew affects both leaves and fruits. Fruit symptoms include a white powdery coating on the skin; brown or buff patches are sometimes present. The fruits will sometimes split if the infection becomes established while they are still small.

Remedy
It is important to spray before the disease becomes established. Apply a fungicide such as carbendazim when the flowers first open, and again a fortnight later.

If a preventive spray hasn't been applied and the vine becomes severely infected, prune out and destroy all affected fruit and foliage.

Scab
The two common fruit scabs are apple scab and pear scab. Although they are caused by different fungi, they present similar symptoms and require much the same treatment.

The fruit is disfigured by dark-coloured scabby blemishes (similar spots occur on the leaves but are greener in appearance). Badly affected fruits will be small and mis-shapen or cracked.

Remedy
To remove a source of future infection, rake up fallen leaves and fruit, and dispose of them without delay. Spray with a fungicide such as bupirimate with triforine, carbendazim or mancozeb. Start spraying at bud burst and repeat at intervals (for detailed advice regarding a particular chemical, follow the instructions on the container).

If scab is an annual problem, try growing varieties that show some resistance to the disease. Among resistant apples are 'Discovery' and 'Sunset' — among the pears 'Catillac' and 'Jargonelle'. You should never store affected fruit.

Tomato blight
Blight usually affects the foliage first (see the description on page 72), but the fruits show a brown discoloration and may shrink or rot.

Remedy
See page 72 for advice on control.

Flower problems

Botrytis (grey mould)

This ubiquitous fungal disease (see also page 78) lives on both living and dead tissue, and dying flowers are often affected, especially in damp weather. The disease can spread to flowers in bloom or bud. In mild cases the petals are simply spotted, but if the condition becomes severe, the flowers may rot prematurely.

Remedy

Deadheading will reduce the problem. Fungicides such as carbendazim will control *Botrytis*, but flowers are so transient that they are probably not worth spraying.

Petal blight

Flowers such as chrysanthemums are sometimes affected by petal blight — a fungal disease that produces brown marks on the petals. In severe cases the whole flower may rot prematurely.

Remedy

Pick off and destroy affected flowers. If the plants are under glass, reduce the humidity levels and make sure there is plenty of ventilation.

A fungicide such as mancozeb will help to control the problem, but in most cases is not really necessary.

Botrytis cinerea *will affect flowers and foliage where air circulation is poor and conditions damp. This African violet (*Saintpaulia) has *succumbed because it was left in a sleeve for too long.*

Rhododendron bud blast

Azaleas and rhododendrons are prone to this fungal disease, which causes the buds to remain closed and undeveloped. They often assume a silvery-grey colour, and are later covered with bristle-like black fungal fruiting bodies.

Remedy

Pick off and destroy affected buds as soon as you notice them. In future years, keep leaf hoppers under control (see page 45), as these insects spread the disease.

Tulip fire

If tulips have bleached spots on the petals or the flowers don't open properly, they may be suffering from tulip fire. This is especially likely if the foliage is streaked and stunted. See page 76 for a full description and advice on control.

Viruses

Viruses can cause streaks and flashes of different colours in petals. See page 77 for more information about virus diseases.

Fungi growing on tree trunks are generally a warning that all may not be well. There are many fungi that grow on trees, and they often indicate that the tree is in a poor state of health. If in doubt you are advised to consult a tree surgeon.

Stem problems

Botrytis (grey mould)
This common disease affects stems as it does most other parts of the plant, but less so than leaves and flowers (see previous page). The stem becomes discoloured, usually with a fuzzy grey growth on the surface.

Remedy
Prune out affected stems.

Bracket fungi
There are several kinds of bracket-like fungi grow on the trunks and branches of trees. They are sometimes an indication of a deteriorating tree,

and over a period of years they can cause damage by weakening the structure of a limb or trunk. Bracket fungi should be regarded as a potential indicator that the tree is not in good condition internally.

Remedy
Simply cutting or breaking off the external parts of the fungi will have little effect. Consult a tree surgeon if in doubt about the health of the tree and the risk posed by the fungi.

Clematis wilt
This is one of several common wilt diseases (see also overleaf)

caused by a range of different fungi. In this case the stems appear to wilt or the leaves turn brown as if the stem has been severed.

Control
Cut back affected stems well back into healthy tissue. If the attack is mild, the plant may reshoot from lower down. If necessary, cut down to soil level, then give the plant an opportunity to regrow.

Deep planting is sometimes advocated so that plants attacked by clematis wilt will have more chance of regrowing from the base.

Coral spot
The bright orange-red raised pustules of this fungal disease can often be seen on dead wood, but if it becomes established on stems that have die-back, or on pruned stumps, the infection may spread into healthy tissue.

Remedy
Prune out affected shoots, cutting well back into healthy tissue, and then burn the prunings.

Rusts
Rusts usually affect leaves (see page 74), but sometimes the orange or brown pustules develop on the stems too. In severe cases the stem becomes distorted.

Remedy
See page 74 for the control of rusts.

Wilt

Wilts affect a wide range of plants and are caused by a variety of fungi, though the most significant are the *Fusarium* and *Verticillium* groups. The first indications may be discoloration of the leaves as if the plant is dry, but then in some cases the whole stem collapses as if severed at the base.

Plants affected include asters, peonies and of course clematis. See the preceding page for clematis wilt, page 66 for *Fusarium* wilt, and page 68 for *Verticillium* wilt.

'Sweet Dream' is an outstanding patio rose that is not especially disease-prone. It will succumb to rose black spot (see pages 71–2), and in severe cases all the leaves will be shed. But it should grow back readily the following spring, and will remain healthy if you spray routinely as a precaution.

Nutritional and physiological problems

Not all plant problems are due to pests or diseases. Problems that look like a disease may often be due to nutritional deficits, such as iron and manganese deficiencies. A plant that has collapsed, and looks as though it has a root disease, may in fact be suffering from no more than water-logged soil.

If, after careful checking, you can find no trace of a pest and there isn't a disease that appears to explain the symptoms fully, then you should consider the possibility of a nutritional deficiency or some kind of physiological cause.

Nutritional deficiencies

Most deficiencies reveal themselves in the colour of the foliage as well as in overall vigour, but some of them are difficult to distinguish simply from the foliage.

If you suspect a major nutrient deficiency, try a soil test kit — this will give some indication of whether the soil is significantly short of nitrogen, phosphorus or potassium.

Simple kits for the gardener will not detect deficiencies in the minor nutrients — so-called trace elements — which are nevertheless vitally important. On the other hand, fertilisers containing all the vital trace elements are readily available, so try using one of these and see whether there is any improvement.

If the soil is very alkaline — chalky soil, for example — some of the trace elements, especially iron and manganese, are often unavailable to the majority of plants. Applying ordinary trace elements may not help, as they quickly become 'locked' by the soil, but so-called chelated or sequestered products are available to overcome this.

Physiological disorders

Suspect these if the weather has recently been extreme in some way. Hail will cause obvious physical damage, high winds will 'burn' even quite tough foliage (especially in coastal areas), and long periods of rain or drought carry their own obvious risks.

There's nothing drastically wrong with this Impatiens. *It's just been planted out without careful hardening off (acclimatisation), with the result that the leaves have been scorched by the sun.*

Nutritional deficiencies

Apple bitter pit

The name of this disorder, which is normally caused by calcium deficiency, is highly descriptive: the skin of the fruit is pitted and the brown-flecked flesh tastes bitter. Sometimes the symptoms develop while the fruits are in store.

Remedy

Calcium deficiency is a complex disorder. There may, for example, be sufficient calcium in the soil, but without adequate moisture it is not available to the plant. Too much calcium may also cause similar symptoms.

In future, make sure the tree does not suffer from drought, and use a balanced fertiliser in spring to ensure strong growth. The fruit can be sprayed with a calcium nitrate solution through the summer and into autumn, but this is seldom worth considering for a few garden trees, and some varieties can be damaged by the chemical.

Boron deficiency

This is a very rare deficiency that sometimes occurs if the soil has been very heavily limed, or if light soils have been subject to flooding. It is most likely to happen to vegetable crops.

Boron deficiency may become apparent when you

Bitter pit is a problem found in apples that is usually due to a shortage of calcium.

cut open root vegetables such as parsnips, swedes and turnips, where it produces a characteristic brown discoloration, often in concentric rings, and there are sometimes cavities too. Beetroot may suffer from internal discoloration. Carrots tend to split, sometimes down to the central core, and the foliage may look pinkish or yellow. Cauliflowers develop poor curds, which may turn brown.

Remedy

If boron deficiency occurs on the vegetable plot, you should apply borax to the soil before sowing, at a rate of approximately 2 g/m². This is an extremely small amount, so you should bulk it up with dry sand to make sure that it is evenly applied.

Iron and manganese deficiencies

These deficiencies often occur when lime-hating plants are grown in alkaline (chalky) soil (see picture below).

The leaf veins remain green, but the area between them becomes pale and yellow; sometimes the leaves are also brown along the edges. The symptoms usually start at the edges of the leaves and spread over most of the leaf, between the veins. The plant fails to

These sick-looking bergenias are not suffering from any disease — they have an iron and manganese deficiency resulting from the very alkaline soil they are growing in.

thrive. Unlike with magnesium deficiency (see below), the youngest leaves are usually affected, the older ones less so.

Remedy

If the plants are in containers, replant them in an ericaceous (acid) potting compost. In beds and borders, apply the missing elements in chelated or fritted form, or else use sequestered iron. All these items will be available from a good garden centre.

Magnesium deficiency

This deficiency often occurs on very acid soils, or after flooding or periods of heavy rain, as magnesium is easily leached from the ground.

*This neglected rubber plant (*Ficus elastica*) shows signs of nitrogen deficiency as well as the effects of poor light.*

The leaves look as though they are ageing prematurely, with small yellow or brown patches between the leaf veins. Sometimes the brown areas have a yellow edge, worse on older leaves. The leaves often fall prematurely.

All kinds of plants may be affected, but chrysanthemums, roses and tomatoes are especially likely to suffer from magnesium deficiency.

Remedy

Epsom salts will rectify the problem. Apply this to the soil at a rate of 1 oz per sq yd (25 g/m²). For quicker results, use as a foliar feed by diluting 7 oz of Epsom salts in 2 gallons of water (210 g in 10 l). Add a wetting agent, such as a few drops of washing-up liquid.

Nitrogen deficiency

This is the commonest nutrient deficiency as the element is readily leached out of the soil,

but it is also the easiest to correct. The leaves are smaller and paler than normal. Sometimes red or purple colours show through, though this only happens on some plants. A simple soil test kit that includes a nitrogen test will readily confirm the diagnosis.

Remedy

Apply a quick-acting nitrogenous fertiliser such as sulphate of ammonia or dried blood to the soil, or use a high-nitrogen liquid feed. Then use a soil test kit to determine a strategy for raising the long-term fertility of your soil.

Phosphate deficiency

It is uncommon for plants to be starved of phosphates, but the problem may occur in

Physiological disorders

Drought

Because water is so essential to all the vital physical and chemical life-support mechanisms that keep a plant healthy, drought will create both immediate and long-term problems.

Drooping leaves and wilting stems are the first sign of water shortage, but if the drought is persistent the foliage may eventually turn brown and papery. If trees and shrubs are affected, the autumn colours may arrive early, and many plants roll their leaves in an attempt to reduce water loss.

Flower buds may fail to open properly, or the blooms may be sparse and small. Fruits are usually small and may be distorted in shape.

Lack of moisture may cause calcium deficiency in tomatoes, leading to blossom end rot — though this is normally only found when they are grown in containers or under glass. A dark, sunken area develops at the bottom of the fruits, which gradually becomes larger and leathery in texture.

Remedy

Irrigate your plants before symptoms become advanced, but water heavily and less frequently rather than little and often, which may cause

areas of high rainfall and on acid soil. Suspect phosphate deficiency if growth is slow and the leaves look unnaturally dull with an abnormal yellowy tinge. A soil test should confirm the diagnosis.

Remedy

Apply superphosphate or bonemeal, bearing in mind that both of these are slow-acting and should be applied in early spring. If a balanced general fertiliser is used routinely, this should provide sufficient superphosphate along with the other main nutrients.

Potassium deficiency

This mainly causes poor flowering and fruiting, but

These pansies are under stress, suffering badly from the effects of drought.

there may be leaf symptoms too. The tips or edges of the leaves may look reddish or scorched, and there may be brownish-purple spotting on the underside.

Remedy

Potassium deficiency can be easily corrected by applying sulphate of potash.

This procedure is usually carried out in spring, but if you use a high-potash liquid feed, such as one intended for tomatoes in fruit, this will give a quick boost during the growing season.

surface rooting and aggravate the problem.

Mulching will help to conserve moisture, but you should only mulch ground that is already moist.

Frost and wind burn

The leaves turn brown or black, and hang or look withered. Often only the ends or edges of the leaves are affected. Biting cold winter winds have a similar effect on evergreens. Suspect wind or frost damage if the symptoms follow severe weather.

Early flowers may sometimes be damaged by frost even when the plant itself is totally hardy. Camellias are often spoiled if the sun thaws the frozen petals too rapidly. Signs of frost damage include brown petals, often just at the most exposed tips.

Remedy

You can prune out frosted leaves if they look unsightly. But provided the plant is hardy, new growth will usually hide the damaged foliage.

Vulnerable plants can sometimes be protected from late frosts by draping environmental netting or horticultural fleece over them until the risk is past. If you plant early-flowering blooms such as camellias in a position that remains shaded for the first few hours of daylight, this may stop them thawing so rapidly and thus minimise the potential damage.

Irregular watering

Drought and waterlogging aren't the only water-related problems. Irregular watering also stresses the plant. Some leaves may become distorted and puckered, and fruits (especially tomatoes) may split. This is because the skin initially becomes hard and tough through lack of water, and then cannot expand readily enough when a plentiful supply of water is available. With woody plants, the bark may crack or split.

Remedy

The problem is seldom worth worrying about outdoors, as every season is different. Under glass, you need to be careful not to let the soil or compost dry out — an automatic watering system is a good solution.

Heavy rain

In very wet weather, flowers sometimes rot before they open. Some roses are particularly prone to a condition known as balling. The buds fail to open, with the outer petals turning brown and papery — and if the damp weather persists, the whole bud eventually rots. The problem is often worse when hot sun follows prolonged rain.

Remedy

Simply cut off affected buds before they begin to rot. Some varieties are more susceptible than others, so if you grow a

If very mild weather in early spring is followed by a late frost, new foliage may be damaged on vulnerable plants. This one is a hydrangea; the plant will easily outgrow the setback.

plant that is vulnerable, avoid overhead watering during the hot, sunny part of the day.

Scorch

Pale or dark-brown patches, or sometimes bleached-looking blotches, may occur on foliage when excessive heat is concentrated on small areas of a particular leaf or of sections of foliage. This can happen when drops of water act like a lens and concentrate the sun's rays, which is one reason why it's always best to water plants in the evening.

Often the culprit is window or greenhouse glass. Patterned glass is especially harmful to houseplants, as the rays can be intensified even more, and may cause long brown streaks to appear where the intensified rays have fallen as the sun has moved across the sky.

Remedy

You should always make sure that greenhouses and conservatories are shaded and well ventilated. In the home, only place really tough plants such as cacti and pelargoniums near to the glass in an unshaded window. Even a net curtain may be enough to help protect plants on a windowsill.

Above *Pale-golden leaves like those on this* Philadelphus coronarius 'Aureus' *may be scorched by strong sun. It's best to grow such a plant in a well-lit position that is out of the direct sun during the hottest part of the day*

Right *This* Stromanthe sanguinea *is not suffering from a disease — just from being placed too close to patterned glass. The sun has scorched the leaves through the glass, creating a banding effect as it moved across the sky.*

Waterlogging

If poorly drained ground becomes waterlogged for long periods, this will eventually have adverse effects on plants that are vulnerable to over-watering. Pot plants will show the same symptoms if you overwater them.

The plant wilts as though underwatered, and the leaves slowly turn yellow. When the plant is lifted, the roots may look abnormally black, or may even have rotted.

Remedy

If the problem is persistent, you should improve drainage by laying land drains, and improve the structure of the soil by adding gritty material

Proliferation

This abnormal growth pattern manifests itself when flower buds form within an existing flower. They usually remain as unopened buds, but sometimes they grow into stems with more flowers, and occasionally they may even have leaves too. The problem is most often seen in roses, but it may also occur with other plants, such as apples and pears.

The likely cause of proliferation is damage to the emerging growing tip of the bud, perhaps as a result of insect attack. If the same plant keeps producing proliferated flowers, it is even possible that a virus is responsible.

If a regular recurrence of the problem leads you to suspect that a virus is involved, you should lift and destroy the plant. Otherwise just prune out the affected shoot.

and plenty of organic matter. For a small area, raising the bed slightly may be sufficient to improve matters.

When pot plants have been affected by overwatering, you should remove them from their pots, wrap the root-ball in newspaper or kitchen paper to absorb as much moisture as possible, then leave them exposed to the air to dry. You should then repot them, keep them out of direct sunlight for a few days, then water them only cautiously.

Weedkiller damage

Weedkiller spray drift can cause a wide range of plant symptoms, depending on the particular chemical used and the plant affected.

Path weedkillers applied carelessly may cause yellowing of the foliage of nearby plants.

Hormone lawn weedkillers may cause broad-leaved plants to develop distorted leaves, which may curl in around the edges, becoming slightly cup-shaped. Stems may become distorted, or small bumps may appear on them. Fruits may also change shape — round tomatoes may become almost plum-shaped.

Remedy

Slightly affected plants may well grow out of trouble. If not, you should lift and discard them, and be more careful next time you apply a weed-killer to the lawn.

Never mulch beds with grass clippings from a lawn that has recently been treated with a weedkiller, and be careful about using compost that may still contain the residues of plants treated with a weedkiller. (There are some weed-killers that break down quickly on contact with the soil and will not cause a problem if composted.)

Weedkiller spray drift damage usually manifests itself as scorch-like marks, though the exact symptoms will depend on the type of weedkiller involved. If this kind of damage occurs within a few days of spraying, there is probably a connection.

Fasciation

This rather strange disorder may be due to variety of factors, such as damage to the growing tip from insect or frost attack, a bacterial or viral infection, or simply a genetic defect.

Affected shoots or flowers have broad, flattened stems, and often look as though two have become fused into one. The stem or stalk usually becomes distorted. The problem can affect many different plants.

Although fasciation looks like a serious problem, the plant will come to no harm. If you find the affected stem or flower interesting, then just leave it. If you don't like it, simply prune it out.

Flowers as well as stems can be fasciated. The one you see here is a fasciated narcissus.

A healthy lawn

Lawns are not especially prone to pests or diseases, and poor grass is more likely to be due to lack of feeding and perhaps poor drainage. However, as problems are often specific to lawns when they do occur, all the common lawn pests, diseases and animal problems have been grouped together in this section.

Bear in mind that pest and disease control should often be accompanied by cultural changes too, such as feeding or aerating the lawn.

Algae
Slippery patches of green or blackish slimy growth are likely to be caused by algae, which are often an indication of a poorly drained and badly aerated lawn.

Remedy
A moss killer such as one based on dichlorophen is likely to help in the short term. But if you want to prevent the problem recurring in future, you should also improve the drainage of your lawn and aerate the surface.

Bitches urinating on the lawn will cause scorched brown patches like this one. You can reduce the damage by flushing the area with water to dilute the urine.

Ants
Ants are not only a nuisance for anyone sitting on the grass, but they also produce heaps of fine soil on the surface above their nests. This in turn may interfere with mowing and provide a place for weed seeds to germinate.

Remedy
Knock the heaps away with a broom or besom, then try watering the nest area with an insecticide such as carbaryl, chlorpyrifos or pyrethrum.

Drought
The symptoms of drought require no description. Most gardeners are alas only too familiar with the all-over lack of green colouring as the leaves turn brown.

Remedy
The remedy is equally obvious, but the watering method used can make a difference. Watering little and often may mean the water doesn't penetrate very far, and this can make matters worse by encouraging shallow rooting. Use sufficient water to penetrate several inches, even if this means applying it less often.

A brown lawn may look unattractive, but in times of water shortages it should be a low priority for a scarce resource. The grass will rapidly grow again once the rain returns.

Dogs
Dogs, and particularly bitches, cause brown patches by urinating on the lawn.

Remedy
Whenever possible, flush the area with water to dilute the urine before it can scorch the

grass. Dogs can usually be trained to use another area.

Dollar spot

This fungus disease causes small pale-brown patches to appear in early autumn. At first they are only a couple of inches (a few centimetres) across, but they eventually coalesce to form large patches.

Remedy

Rake the lawn with a lawn rake, and improve the aeration with an aerator. Treat the affected areas with an appropriate fungicide such as carbendazim.

Earthworms

These creatures are generally beneficial to gardens because they help to aerate the soil. On the other hand, they can spoil a lawn if they produce too many worm casts — small, muddy deposits of soil on the surface.

Remedy

Suitable worm killers are not available to amateurs at the present time, and in any case you should not resort to killing earthworms unless the number of casts is excessive. The casts can be brushed away easily when dry.

Fairy rings

Certain fungi that live in grass produce toadstools in the autumn, often creating a ring formation as fungal threads within the ground spread outwards. The toadstools are often accompanied by a couple of circles of lush and very green grass, while the grass between them grows poorly.

Fairy rings, which are difficult to eliminate, are most disfiguring when they appear on high-quality ornamental lawns.

Remedy

There are no suitable chemical controls available to amateurs

at the time of writing, but you can brush off the toadstools before they can shed their spores. If fairy rings are really a problem, you can attempt to eliminate the disease by digging out the affected grass, plus an area 1 ft (30 cm) beyond the known extent of the problem, to a depth of at least 1 ft (30 cm). You should then fill the hole with fresh soil and reseed. Dispose of the excavated soil where it will not pose a threat to other lawns.

Leatherjackets
These grey-brown legless grubs — the larvae of the familiar daddy-long-legs — can be a

Fairy rings on a lawn are produced by a fungus colony growing outwards in a widening circle.

particular problem in lawns, where they feed on the roots of the grass. The visible symptoms are brown patches in the lawn in midsummer.

If you explore around the roots you should eventually find the larvae. Otherwise, soak the grass and cover the area with a piece of black polythene overnight and then check for their presence.

Remedy
If you want to avoid chemicals, try the black polythene technique described above, then remove the sheet in the morning and handpick or allow the birds to feast on them. There is also a possibility of a biological control. Alternatively, you could water on an insecticide such as carbaryl, chlorpyrifos or pyrethrum.

Molehills are unsightly and can ruin the appearance of a lawn. If the number of moles responsible is relatively small, then smoke cones and traps should succeed in eliminating the problem.

Moles
Molehills — ugly heaps of soil created by the burrowing activity of moles — can ruin the appearance of a lawn, and in ornamental turf they will almost certainly require attention.

Remedy
Smoke cones and electronic devices may have some limited success, but trapping is usually the preferred method. Mole traps can be bought from good garden centres.

Red thread

This lawn disease is caused by a fungus that produces pink to red threads among the grass, which can be seen on close examination. The grass may become bleached in the affected area but is rarely killed.

Remedy

To combat red thread, it is usually sufficient to improve the lawn by cultural methods. Scarify and aerate the grass, and feed the lawn regularly in spring and summer to stimulate vigorous growth.

If the problem is severe enough to require chemical treatment, then use a fungicide such as carbendazim.

Snow mould (*Fusarium* patch)

This lawn disease is caused by a fungus that turns the grass yellow in patches, which may coalesce to form larger areas. In damp weather a white fungal growth may be visible. The disease is worst in late autumn and winter, especially if the grass has been covered with snow.

Remedy

Treat the affected grass with a fungicide such as carbendazim. To reduce the risk of the disease returning in future years, you should scarify and aerate the lawn regularly, and try not to apply high doses of nitrogenous fertilisers.

Above *A well-groomed lawn can help to make an impressive garden; one full of brown patches caused by disease will be an embarrassment. It's well worth taking lawn pests and diseases seriously, and acting promptly to deal with them.*

Right Fusarium *patches like these need to be treated with a suitable fungicide.*

Index

adelgids 55
aerosols 28-9
algae 91
Amblyseius 8
American gooseberry mildew 69, 78
animals 57-62
antirrhinums 26
ants 91
Aphidius 8, 12
Aphidoletes 12
aphids 10, 41-3, 55, 56
apple bitter pit 84
apple capsids 50

Bacillus thuringiensis 7, 13, 43
bacteria 11-12, 71
barriers 20-23
beetles
    flea 44
    ground 19
    lily 46, 53-4
    raspberry 51-2
biological warfare 6-10
birds 10, 20, 35, 60-62
black spot 71-72, 82
blackbirds 60
blackfly *see* aphids
boron deficiency 84
Botrytis 69, 78, 80, 81
bracket fungi 81
brown rot 78-9
bulbs *see* root problems
bullfinches 60-61
butterflies 43

cabbage root fly 22, 37
cages 20, 21, 61
calcium deficiency 84
capsid bugs 43, 50, 63
carrot fly 23, 37
caterpillars 43
cats 58
chafer grubs 37-8
chemicals 6-7, 27-31
    names 28
chocolate spot 69-70
clematis wilt 81
cloches 22
clubroot 65
codling moths 16, 51
collar barriers 22
contact insecticides 27, 28
coral spot 81

crop rotation 35
Cryptolaemus 13
cuckoo spit 55
cutworms 38

dahlias 29, 53, 94
damping off 65
deer 21, 59
deficiencies *see* nutritional problems
Delphastus 13, 14
dips 31
diseases 64-82
disposal of material 32, 34-5
dogs 58, 91-2
dollar spot 92
downy mildew 70-71
drought 86-7, 91
dusts 28, 31

earthworms 92
earwigs 18, 43-4, 53
eelworms *see* nematodes
Encarsia 14

fairy rings 92-3
fasciation 90
fieldfares 62
fireblight 71
flea beetles 44
fleeces 22
flower problems 53-4, 80
foot rots 65-6
froghoppers 55
frogs 10
frost burn 87
fruit problems 26, 50-53, 78-9
fungal diseases 32, 64-82
fungicides 30-31
fungus gnat 38
Fusarium 66, 71, 94

galls 38, 44
grease bands 33
greenfly *see* aphids
grey mould 69, 78, 80, 81

hardening off 83
hares 60
Heterorhabditis 14
honey fungus 66
honeysuckle aphids 42
hoverflies 10
hygiene 34, 35
Hypoaspis 15

INDEX

identifying pests 36
insecticides 7, 27-9
introduction 4
iron deficiency 84-5

ladybirds 7, 10, 13
lawn problems 91-4
leaf-cutting bees 45
leaf hoppers 45
leaf miners 45
leaf problems 41-50, 69-77
leaf spot 71-2
leatherjackets 39, 93
Leptomastix 15
lily beetle 46, 53-4

magnesium deficiency 85
manganese deficiency 84-5
mealybugs 13, 15, 40, 46, 55
Metaphycus 15
mice 19, 59
mildew
　American gooseberry 69, 78
　downy 70-71
　powdery 73, 79
mites 15
　red spider 11, 46-7
moles 93
moths 43
　codling 16, 51
　winter 33
mould
　grey 69, 78, 80, 81
　snow 94
　sooty 42, 75
　tomato leaf 76

narcissus eelworms 39
natural predators 9-16
nematodes 5, 11-12, 14, 15, 39
netting 20-21, 22
nitrogen deficiency 85
nutritional problems 83-6

onion fly 40
ornamental plants 26

pansies 62
pansy sickness 66-7, 72
peach leaf curl 33, 72
pencils 29
pets 57-8
pheromone traps 16-17
phosphate deficiency 85-6
physiological disorders 83, 86-90
Phytophthora 67
pests 36-56
petal blight 80
Phytoseiulus 11, 15
pigeons 62

pins 29
plum moths 51
potassium deficiency 86
potato blight 68, 72-3
potato scab 68
powdery mildew 73, 79
predators 9-16
　purchasing 11-12
pre-empting pests 33
proliferation 89

rabbits 21, 60
rain damage 87
raspberry beetle 51-2
rats 59
red spider mites 11, 15, 46-7
red thread 94
redwings 62
repellents 24
resistant varieties 25-6
rhododendron bud blast 80
root aphids *see* aphids
root problems 37-40, 65-8
root rots 65-6, 67
roses 25, 72, 82
rotation 35
rust diseases 74, 81

sawflies 47, 50-51
scab 68, 74, 79
scale insects 48, 56
scarers 24
sciarid fly 38
scorch 88
shothole 74, 75
silver leaf 75
slugs 15, 17, 23, 40, 48-9, 52, 54
slugworms 47
smoke cones 28-9
smuts 75
snails 18, 23, 48-9, 52, 54
snow mould 94
sooty mould 42, 75
sparrows 61
spider mites 11, 15, 46-7
spray chemicals 28, 31
squirrels 60
Steinernema 15-16
stem problems 55-6, 81-2
sticky traps 19, 23
storage rots 68
systemic insecticides 27-8

tactics and strategies 32-5
thrips 49, 54
toadstools 92-3
tomato blight 72-3, 79
tomato leaf mould 76
traps 17-19

tubers *see* root problems
tulip fire 76, 80

vegetables 25
Verticillium 68, 76
vine weevils 8, 12, 40, 49
viruses 77, 80
voles 59

wasps 19, 52-3
　parasitic 12, 14
watering problems 86, 87
waterlogging 89
weather factors 31
weedkiller damage 89-90
weevils, vine 8, 12, 40, 49
whitefly 14, 50
wilt 66, 68, 77, 81, 82
wind burn 87
winter moths 33
wireworms 40-41
wood pigeons 62
woodlice 41
woolly aphids 56